Educating

Gifted

Students

in Middle

School

a p r a c t i c a l g u i d e

Educating Gifted Students in Middle School

a practical guide

Susan Rakow

PRUFROCK PRESS, INC.

Rakow, Susan, 1949-
   Educating gifted students in middle school : a practical guide.
      p. cm.
   Includes bibliographical references.
   ISBN 1-59363-164-2
   1. Gifted children—Education (Middle school)—United States.
   I. Title.

   LC3993.23.R35 2005
   371.95'72—dc22

                                               2005016524

Printed in the United States of America.

At the time of this book's publication, all facts and figures cited are the most current available. All telephone numbers, addresses, and Web site URLs are accurate and active. All publications, organizations, Web sites, and other resources exist as described in the book, and all have been verified. The authors and Prufrock Press, Inc., make no warranty or guarantee concerning the information and materials given out by organizations or content found at Web sites, and we are not responsible for any changes that occur after this book's publication. If you find an error, please contact Prufrock Press, Inc.

Prufrock Press, Inc.
P.O. Box 8813
Waco, Texas 76714-8813
(800) 998-2208
Fax (800) 240-0333
http://www.prufrock.com

This book is dedicated
to the students, faculty, parents, and principal
of Beachwood Middle School,
whose support, intelligence, patience, and questions
allowed me to follow my passion
to improve education
for middle school gifted students.

Table of Contents

Acknowledgements

Nothing happens in a vacuum. Countless connections with other books, scholars, friends, students, and family change the way we think and act. For all those who have helped me grow and think, I am profoundly grateful.

Special gratitude—

To Gordon Vars, an extraordinary mentor and friend whose life is a model of scholarly accomplishment and dedication to humanitarian values.

To Jim Kendrick and Joel McIntosh at Prufrock Press, who accepted and supported the need for this book .

To my parents, Betty and George Bosnick, who gave me the confidence to accept life's challenges.

To my children, Josh and Becca, whose gifts have illuminated my life and fueled my passion to make change for others.

To Benjamin, my first grandchild, because he is the future for whom this book is written.

And, most of all, to my husband, Larry, because without him in my life, I'd probably still be a wannabe cheerleader.

Introduction

Ever since I completed my dissertation in 1993 on middle school gifted programs, I expected that someone else would write this book: a practical guide to serving gifted students during their middle school years. But, no one has, and there continues to be a rift between the fields of middle school education and gifted education that has been exacerbated by the passage of the No Child Left Behind Act, the publication of *Turning Points 2000*, and other movements toward accountability and minimum competency assessments (e.g., state proficiency tests). Little has been done on a broad scale to bridge the gap with thorough, realistic, and well-supported approaches to understanding and meeting gifted students' needs. Teachers, principals, and gifted coordinators need background information, instructional strategies, programs models, and curriculum ideas that enable and motivate them to provide a more effective match between gifted students and their middle school experiences and environments.

As professionals, educators don't shy away from tackling students' deficits when they are the result of societal failures; our approach is that every student is important, regardless of the reasons he or she is struggling. And we redouble our efforts. The reasons why gifted students exist are almost equally irrelevant to addressing their problems: inequities in home life and experiences, undeserved advantages bestowed by race or class, genes, exceptional drive and motivation. We don't know what part of intelligence is due to nature or nurture. By middle school, the primary challenge is to understand the needs of all of our students—and this includes the gifted—and address them, no matter how we may feel about how they got to be exceptional.

This does not, however, let gifted advocates off the social-justice hook. We must simultaneously work to change any forces that may have created these disparities and ensure that assessment, identification, and resources are culturally responsive and fair. We need to work as collaborative partners in creating middle schools that are effective for all, including the gifted.

Many aspects of sound middle school philosophy are part of good gifted education and vice versa. Both believe that schools should:

- provide active, engaging, and personally relevant learning experiences that include high expectations and intellectual challenge, as well as basic skills and opportunities to explore for all students;
- use curricula that are interdisciplinary, integrated, and theme-based;
- be based on understanding of early adolescents' unique needs and wide range of cognitive and affective development;
- provide support that allows each student to progress at an individually appropriate pace;
- involve families and communities as partners in students' educational choices and activities;
- promote self-understanding, acceptance, and positive identity development;
- use a variety of instructional strategies and materials to meet students' varying needs and abilities, including large- and small-group activities and individualized independent work;

- have specially trained, well-prepared professionals who understand and act on their roles as student advocates;
- provide safe and supportive environments for all students; and
- use equitable and ongoing assessment and evaluation procedures to influence classroom teaching and decisions about student learning opportunities, including opportunities for student self-assessment.

Unfortunately, black-and-white thinking on both sides has often stood in the way of applying these commonalities to services for gifted students during a key transition in their lives. Parents' horror stories about trying to get services for their gifted children in middle school are legion, even if they have been well served through a range of programming alternatives in responsive elementary schools.

In 1995, Carol Tomlinson's publication *Gifted Learners and the Middle School: Problem or Promise?* described the tension between the two groups. Identified problems included excellence versus equity orientations, emphasis on heterogeneity versus homogeneous grouping and differentiation, the use of labels, debate about good middle school curricula and good gifted curricula, use of cooperative learning, and differing emphases and perceptions of the needs of early adolescents. She also identified their shared beliefs, as well as promising directions of dialogue.

In the hopes of expanding this dialogue, the National Middle School Association (NMSA) published *Dilemmas in Talent Development in the Middle Grades: Two Views* in 1997. However well intentioned, it ultimately did little but provide a platform for the two opposing schools of thought. Tom Erb's thoughtful introduction to the conflict expresses his hope that the book would provide both divergent opinions and

a clearer view . . . about how educators can work together to provide the curricular and instructional differentiation necessary to challenge all learners and to do this without resorting to the hyperspecialization that proved so problematic in factory-model junior high schools characterized by departmentalization and IQ-based gifted programs. (p. 6)

He confesses, however, that many schools calling themselves middle schools are not using the best middle school elements and strategies, including teaming.

Throughout the book, Paul George of NMSA asserts that services for students identified as gifted are an undeserved privilege that drains resources from other more needy (and therefore, in his view, more deserving) students. His firm antigrouping stance barely moves toward accepting the possibilities of flexible grouping. Instead, he promotes differentiation in the general education classroom as an effective heterogeneous way to meet gifted students' "reasonable" needs. George continues to disparage gifted advocates for "misinterpreting" evidence and research on ability grouping, middle schools, and gifted programs. He asserts that their criticisms have undermined confidence in the public schools as a whole and goes so far as to say that "asking the schools to organize and operate so as to provide enrichment or acceleration beyond a curriculum which provides a uniform education may be unconstitutional" (p. 34). He accuses gifted advocates of "playing into the hands of those who would dismantle our public schools" (p. 6). George trivializes concern for the gifted by saying that "educators have more urgent concerns which require the concerted energy and commitment of all of us" (p. 11) and states that gifted advocates don't care about anyone else. He asserts the value of curriculum compacting while admitting that most teachers don't know what it is or how to do it. Research and my own experience with hundreds of classroom teachers supports this last observation.

Joseph Renzulli and Sally Reis offer the counterpoint chapters supporting the very real needs of gifted and talented students in the current context of broader definitions of giftedness. They offer a critique of current middle school environments and curricula and their unresponsiveness to gifted students. They suggest the use of the Schoolwide Enrichment Model (SEM), as well as some other modest suggestions for change, including a strong plea for open-mindedness and compromise on the grouping issue. They reframe George's view of "privilege" as appropriate and necessary "opportunities." Their concluding chapter mentions the theory-to-practice gap in education, both in gifted education and in middle school.

All in all, *Dilemmas in Talent Development in the Middle Grades* seemed to serve the purpose of lancing a festering boil without, however, curing the systemic infection or healing the wound. Little helpful reconciliation or problem solving was accomplished by this publication, although it provided an essential first step. While all contributors are dedicated and well-respected voices in our profession to whom we can all be grateful, I believe my more than 20 years in middle school classrooms working with gifted students and their teachers and parents offer a realistic and important additional perspective. The equity emphasis of the middle school advocates continues to be portrayed in opposition to the excellence emphasis of gifted advocates, and it is precisely to bridge this gap that I offer this book.

In a more recent publication *The War Against Excellence: The Rising Tide of Mediocrity in America's Middle Schools* (2004), Cheri Pierson Yecke suggests that it is "radical" middle school proponents who have consciously chosen not to address the needs of gifted students; thus, it appears that some middle school advocates have contributed to polarizing the debate and it is *they* who have provided fodder for parents moving their children from public schools to charters, vouchers, and private options. Though Yecke's book in itself is an ultraconservative attack, too many of its allegations ring true to middle school gifted students, their teachers, and their parents. *Genius Denied: How to Stop Wasting Our Brightest Minds* (2004) by Jan and Bob Davidson is a gentler, but no less passionate description of how gifted students are not receiving the education they deserve. They assert that schools' devotion to the lowest common denominator and anti-intellectualism are wasting children's and young adults' talents and time.

In October 2004, a joint position statement was issued by the National Middle School Association and the National Association for Gifted Children calling for action on this issue (see Appendix A). Avoiding the politics of the word *gifted* and following the nationwide trend of switching to "high ability" and "high potential," the statement was entitled *Meeting the Needs of High Ability and High Potential Learners in the Middle Grades*. The report urges implementation of appropriate identification, assessment, and curricular and instructional programs for middle school students with advanced abilities or potential. It concludes with a "Call to Action" for district and school leaders, teachers, gifted education specialists and support personnel, and parents. But, the specifics of implementation are left to be worked out later.

The purpose of this book, then, is to provide teachers, parents, and administrators with an overview of the unique needs of gifted adolescents during fifth to eighth grade, as well as specific guidelines for program and curricular planning. The middle grades should be vital and responsive welcoming communities for *all* students. It is time to move forward and create practical and realistic school solutions that reconcile the two points of view while engaging and challenging gifted students in middle schools.

Nature and Needs of Gifted Middle School Students

Essential Questions

1. In what ways are gifted students different from typical students during their middle school years?

2. Why do gifted students need differentiated accommodations and services during middle school?

Definitions and descriptions of giftedness vary. Volumes have been written about the dimensions of giftedness that go beyond the limited notion of an IQ score as the sole determinant. Current theory and practice are moving toward ever-broadening definitions and revised labels (Erb, 1997).

However, regardless of the definition or multifaceted description that is chosen, it is not debatable that exceptional students whose abilities and talents far surpass what is typical for their age and grade exist in our schools and classrooms. Whether we use Sternberg's triarchic theory, Gardner's ever-increasing multiple intelligences, Renzulli's Talent Portfolio, Terman's narrow definition of the top 1% of measured IQ, outstanding demonstrated creativity and artistic talent, or whatever other approach is in fashion at any given moment, every day classroom teachers face students whose needs are not being met by the typical middle school curriculum, instruction, or school organizational patterns.

Of course, gifted students have some of the same needs as typical middle school students. They are developing meaningful interpersonal relationships, physical comfort with their own changing bodies and evolving sexuality, a personal and social values system, psychologically healthy self-esteem and identity, and increasing independence from and in their families. All adolescents at this age need role models, supportive adults, and appropriate intellectual stimulation to ensure growth. But, gifted adolescents also have unique needs during this period of transition (Buescher & Higham, 2003; Cross, 2004; Rakow 1989).

Gifted students are often significantly more advanced than their peers in one or more academic areas and have a greater propensity for deductive thinking. They have increased ability to observe themselves and to verbalize strong feelings, rather than act on them (Buescher, 1991). Adolescents who have exceptional cognitive abilities also tend to have increased sensitivity to people and events, are more deeply introspective, and often display a higher sense of justice and fair play. Their actions and ideas are often influenced by heightened self-criticism, sensitivity, and intensity (Mendaglio, 2002). Their ability to make a deeper commitment to, or concentrate on, one activity often results in a narrow focus: stamp collecting, mathematics, computers, music, reading, and so forth.

These important personality traits of gifted and talented students are untapped by intelligence tests and are often unacknowledged and misunderstood by those who work with them. These characteristic ways of feeling and acting arise from heightened sensitivities—a different manner of experiencing the world. Dabrowski and Piechowski (1977; Piechowski, 1986) described these enhanced channels of experience in five dimensions or forms of emotional overexcitability: psychomotor, sensual, intellectual, imaginational, and emotional. These contribute to the

individual's psychological development and behaviors, both positive
and negative. For example, the positive and productive side of heightened psychomotor sensitivity is a
surplus of energy marked by rapid
speech, obvious enthusiasm, and a
push for quick action. But, the negative side may manifest as compulsive
talking, workaholism, and perhaps
nervous habits (e.g., tics or nail bit-
ing) that physically express emotional
tension. The positive side of heightened emotional sensitivity is the ability to identify with and feel concern
for others' feelings. But, the negative

"The truly creative mind in any field is no more than this: a human creature born abnormally, inhumanly sensitive.
To him . . .
a touch is a blow,
a sound is a noise,
a misfortune is a tragedy,
a joy is an ecstasy,
a friend is a lover,
a lover is a god,
and failure is death."

—Pearl Buck

side may be intensified self-criticism, feelings of inadequacy or
guilt, and loneliness. These heightened sensitivities may also contribute to feelings of anxiety and stress, though it is important to
note that overexcitability also brings great joy, beauty, compassion,
and creativity (Lind, 2001). Understanding these characteristics
can help guide gifted students toward self-actualizing behaviors
and emotional growth. They need to understand that others may
not share their level of sensitivity or appreciate their reality. They
need to develop relationships with people who take them seriously and have similar awareness.

Gifted adolescents often strive for mature and adult understanding of human problems and values. In this respect, they
often seek out older friends or adults for companionship. Gifted
adolescents have flashes of insight and creative surges. Their
sophisticated abilities to conceptualize, seek alternatives, explore
diverse relationships, and find creative ways of self-expression will
be useful and fulfilling to them once they reach adulthood. But,
during adolescence, these same qualities may create (rather than
solve) some unique problems.

Young gifted people between the ages of 11 and 15 frequently report a range of problems as a result of their abundant gifts: perfectionism, competitiveness, unrealistic appraisal of their gifts, rejection from peers, confusion due to mixed messages about their talents, and parental and social pressures to achieve, as well as problems with unchallenging school programs or increased expectations. (Buescher & Higham, 2003, ¶ 1)

Issues Around Physical Development

Though significant physical changes occur for all adolescents at this time of their lives, for gifted youngsters, this may be the first time they feel out of control. Suddenly at the mercy of irrational forces, they are confused by the impact their hormones have on their bodies, as well as their emotions and moods. Students have many worries about being "normal," and their previously successful use of problem-solving strategies, even mature ones, doesn't work here when they are at the mercy of body chemistry.

Either early or late puberty can magnify problems. Gifted students who talk and think like adults and have adult interests find that early puberty compounds the challenge they face of being expected to behave like adults. Gifted 12-year-olds have many of the emotional and social difficulties of other 12-year-olds regardless of how smart they are. This apparent disconnect among physical, social, emotional, and intellectual maturity, which is known as "asynchronous development," is at the root of many conflicts gifted adolescents face in middle school.

Especially if a student has been accelerated (or grade-skipped), middle school is often the time that physical differences become most noticeable and most important. And physical differences may add to gifted students' already existing sense of being different and separate. Interscholastic athletics take on a bigger role during middle school, and it isn't enough to just participate.

The emphasis has changed to "winning" and "success" with trophies, pep assemblies, and the other trappings of a culture that highly values sports. As a result, participation for gifted students may prove more embarrassing than enjoyable, especially for nonathletic or late-developing boys. Hébert (2004) described this as "managing an image" based on what the society regards as masculine. Healthy exercise and physical activity may then take a backseat to more sedentary cognitive pursuits that may provide more emotional and physical safety. Since exercise is often a release for tension, it is important that students find some physical activity that is relaxing.

Boys and girls experience these dilemmas differently. Boys who are gifted in the visual and performing arts prefer using their bodies as an instrument of expression, rather than in daring physical activities (Clark, 2002). Some may worry about being perceived as effeminate or gay. From the opposite side, gifted girls may be concerned that too much emphasis on and success in competitive athletics will take away from their attractiveness to the opposite sex, and they too are concerned about assumptions that might be made about their sexual orientation. (Chapter 7 further addresses issues of gay, lesbian, and bisexual gifted students in middle school.)

Gifted girls who physically mature early may face pressures to dress and behave in ways that emphasize their sexuality over their intellect and talent. Participation in athletics may be affected particularly in areas like gymnastics, ballet, and skating, where physical maturity affects balance and may influence the competitive edge. Again, there are repercussions in self-concept if a girl has been dedicated to these activities throughout childhood and is faced with losing them in adolescence. This is when eating disorders often develop, when her body has "betrayed" her by developing. (Chapter 7 addresses issues of gifted girls in more depth.)

Overall, it is an imbalance among physical, emotional, social, and intellectual growth that contributes to the conflicts gifted adolescents face.

Social/Emotional Issues

Gifted adolescents' abilities to assimilate information more rapidly and have quicker insights often contribute to challenges in psychosocial adjustment. In elementary school, social acceptance by parents, teachers, and peers is positively connected to school achievement and being smart. But, in middle school, the teacher's approval is less important than peers' approval, which is often contingent on athletic prowess, rapidly changing fads in clothing or music, or belonging to the right clique (Schroeder-Davis 1995). Previously, the rules were clear: Do well in school, get good grades, behave well toward others, and people will like and accept you. In adolescence, the rules are unclear and often unspoken, change frequently without notice, and the penalties for not following them can be harsh and lasting. Again, previously successful logical problem-solving strategies do not always work here for gifted students in the rapidly shifting sands of the middle school social scene (Rakow, 1989).

Gifted students at this age may feel different from their classmates because of their continuing commitment to academic and intellectual interests. Social groups of peers and society at large have a distinct anti-intellectual attitude (Sowell, 2000). "There is distrust for those who want to do their best because excellence makes others feel bad" (Colangelo, 2004). Participation in special or advanced classes may fulfill students' needs for intellectual stimulation, but it may also create social dilemmas. Gifted students may have a hard time finding compatible friends because they often need more than one group—age peers and intellectual peers. Many students find it difficult to straddle or move smoothly between and among groups at this age. The question "Where do I belong?" has many answers, not all of which can be accommodated easily during middle school.

Gifted students in middle school often feel a negative social stigma and lack of appreciation for their unique abilities. As a result, they may retreat from academic achievement in order to be more accepted (e.g., dumbing down, dropping out of certain clubs or activities, underachieving). These concerns and conflicts seem to be particularly intense for gifted girls, the profoundly gifted, and students who have been radically accelerated.

> For both boys and girls, good grades must be earned with seeming ease, because studious habits are often looked on with suspicion and penalized. For girls intelligence is seen as too aggressive, too masculine and for boys, too feminine. These perceptions cause internal conflicts in the gifted [causing self-esteem to plummet]. (Clark, 2002, p. 203)

Gifted students' heightened sensitivities make them more likely to experience stress, even when everything may seem to be going well (Kaplan, 1990). Every new situation or challenge is accompanied by pressure (from within or from outside) to excel. This may be accompanied by concerns of feeling different and of self-doubt—the "imposter syndrome" in which gifted students fear that, at some point, they will be "uncovered" as just ordinary. Students feel they must accept responsibility for constantly meeting high expectations in demanding course loads, sports participation, leadership in school activities, and even part-time jobs. Gifted adolescents who are particularly susceptible to stress are those who believe that they have significant obligations to others, that they have to be the best all the time, that the world is a terrible place to live, that they deserve the best no matter what, or that they can do anything (Genshaft & Broyles, 1991). Stress can interfere with the very activities through which students express their gifts and talents by causing reduced concentration, oversensitivity to criticism, and cloudy thinking, as well as exhaustion.

Gifted students often become aware of their emotional and inner lives and complex moral and relationship issues very early when compared to their age peers (Piechowski, 1986). As they ponder existential questions and look deeply into the purpose of life, it is important to help them distinguish between sometimes uncomfortable intellectual and emotional inquiry and depression. When combined with powerful questioning minds, gifted adolescents' richer awareness and sensitivities offer them possibilities for extraordinary achievement, self-actualization, and eminence.

Gifted students need trained counselors and teachers who are responsive. They often have few readily available adult or peer role models who can help them through the changes they are facing. They receive mixed messages about what it means to be gifted and what society expects of them, which has the effect of narrowing behavior and identity formation (Cross, 2004). They still need guidance as they seek to find a place in the adult world that accepts, values, and enjoys them. They need to learn how to set and choose among goals, how to persevere, and how to accept both challenge and failure. Under the tutelage of supportive and aware adults, discussions and respect for issues such as unintentional nonverbal messages, new ideas and concepts, how experiencing life in ways that are different from others affects them, how to use imagination, acceptable and unacceptable risks, decision making about their learning and living environments, truth seeking, and individual intellectual pursuits can help gifted students understand and accept themselves and promote growth (Lind, 2001).

But, counseling and guidance are not enough.

> Educational modifications, including teacher training, are probably the single most effective way to prevent social and emotional difficulties in gifted students.... Although counseling, extracurricular enrichment, mentorships, and so forth are helpful, they should never be considered an adequate alternative to a responsive and flexible educational environment matched to the level and pace of the student's learning, recognition for excellence of work habits and persistence of effort, and some choice of topic

in accord with individual interests. These are the right of every student. (Robinson, Reis, Neihart, & Moon, 2002, pp. 276–277)

Academic and Intellectual Issues

All middle school students develop intellectually during adolescence. However, gifted students are, by definition, academically and intellectually advanced beyond their typical age and grade-level peers. They are generally more self-motivated to learn and more aware of societal and global issues.

"It's too boring . . . I know this already . . ."

Too many middle schools continue to accept the old and discredited brain periodicity research that states that middle school students *can't* learn abstract or challenging material because their brain development is at a plateau. This research suggests that teachers concentrate on reviewing and applying previously learned material until students reached later adolescence in high school.

Of course, anyone who has worked in middle schools knows this is nonsense. Many middle school students (though obviously not all) are ready for abstract and conceptual learning, and gifted students may have been already involved in it for years. Academic rigor is often lacking when there is an overreliance or inappropriate use of cooperative learning or too widely mixed ability groups. The repetition common in many middle schools' curricula is often boring for most students, but it's deadly for gifted students. It contributes to underachievement and "turning off" to school, which has been exacerbated by recent emphases on competency/proficiency testing. Middle school proponent and scholar Tom Erb confronts this issue for both gifted and typical students in his introduction to *Dilemmas in Talent Development* (1997):

Middle school classrooms are not supposed to be boring, disengaging places. They are to be characterized by integrated curriculum or at least interdisciplinary curriculum where students work at their own paces and at their own levels to produce projects that demonstrate meaningful applications of the knowledge they are acquiring. Students are supposed to be investigating the questions that they themselves are asking about the world and their place in it. They are supposed to be solving problems as they work in interdependent work groups. All of this effort is directed toward producing products and performances for some real audience. Yet we hear time and again that teachers just cannot meet these goals with all the diversity—developmental, academic, and emotional—of students that they encounter in their classrooms. (p. 2)

"You see, I'm not really that smart after all . . ."

In some middle schools, an opposite problem occurs, but with the same result: underachievement. For many gifted students, middle school may be the first time school is difficult. Having "cruised" through elementary school with straight A's often attained with little real effort, the sudden academic challenge is disruptive to students' sense of self-confidence and self-definition as a "smart" person. The approval of teachers and parents was often predicated on this easy academic achievement, and students fear the loss of this outside validation. Those students who were already somewhat perfectionistic feel that, without certain success (defined as earning an A), the work isn't worth doing at all. A kind of paralysis can result, and parents report that their adolescent has "shut down."

Perfectionism has many causes: pressure from teachers and peers, asynchronous development, dysfunctional families, perfectionistic parents, media influences, even birth order. It becomes evident in a student's attitude toward and perception of a situation Despite varying causes, there are common results: procrastination, dichotomous thinking, chronic fear of failure, paralysis, and workaholic syndrome. Perfectionism can worsen during middle school as students conceive of elaborate projects and then lack the time, expertise, or support to complete them the way they initially envisioned. Since it can't be done exactly "right," it never gets done at all or it is left to the last minute, resulting in an inferior product that can be defended because of lack of time or effort spent on it.

This can also contribute to academic underachievement during the middle grades. Teachers often place great value on due dates, specific requirements, and step-by-step project checklists in order to teach work habits; but, for gifted students, these aspects of academia may limit creativity and encourage a conformist ethos of "just follow the directions, get it done, and turn it in on time," rather than fully exploring the learning opportunities presented by the topic or assignment. One middle school student I know wrote her entire history research paper and *then* wrote the 100 required notecards (one fact to a card only!) in order to get full credit for the paper. Without the notecards, full credit wasn't available regardless of the quality of the paper. This student, now at Stanford Medical School, uses the same holistic research and writing strategies, but without having to waste her time on the notecards.

Some gifted students who easily earned A's in elementary school never needed to develop personally appropriate and effective study skills, so they enter middle school without knowing how to study for a test, how to plan and write long-term assignments and papers, and how to manage their time to include studying and homework. The last minute is no longer good enough; many assignments can't be completed the night before or on the bus to school and still receive an A (though some can!). Again, students may begin to believe "If I have to work at it, I must not be that smart."

This is particularly true for gifted students who suddenly enter a full schedule of honors classes, especially those who did not have adequate gifted services in elementary school. Teachers of advanced classes seem to change how an assignment is assessed. Depth, complexity, sophisticated formal writing, and so forth take precedence over how much effort or time went into it, how attractive it is, and how creative it is (fancy covers and fonts, computer animation, etc.). During the middle school transition, teachers may assume that students are aware of and understand these revised evaluation criteria because of their more mature thinking processes. Thus, teachers may neglect to communicate the new expectations clearly, and students are invariably disappointed by their performance evaluation. Rubrics distributed at the same time as an assignment go a long way toward helping students change where they put their efforts.

Apparent Contradiction

It seems as if there's a contradiction here: Middle school is too easy or boring, or it's too hard or challenging. How can it be both?

It's not the student who is the problem; it's the all-too-common poor fit between the student and his or her educational environment, which includes peers, curricula, instruction, and materials. This problem varies by school and sometimes even by individual teacher. A middle school gifted student can be frustrated because the prealgebra class is so difficult and she really should be doing math homework nightly in order to master it. But, she may simultaneously be frustrated because the science class is so boring—all "hands-on" heterogeneous cooperative learning groups working on science material she learned 3 years ago on the Discovery Channel. Nevertheless, the overall effect is the same: underachievement, alienation from school, self-doubt, increased perfectionism, or outright rebellion. The emotional toll of inappropriate attention to the academic and intellectual needs of gifted students during middle school has lasting effects.

Multipotentiality—"An Embarrassment of Riches"

Multipotentiality exists when gifted individuals are equally talented in several diverse areas, including academics, athletics, leadership, and the arts. For them, decision making about course selection, careers, and colleges, as well as day-to-day time management, can create existential dilemmas.

Multipotential gifted students may be fearful about "not living up to their potential." They worry about how to balance their many dreams with realistic consequences of making one choice and leaving others behind. They question whether it is better to do one thing well or attempt to know a lot about many areas. They need assurance that their many talents are an asset, not a liability and that, in most areas, these decisions do not have to be made in middle school (although in some areas, such as gymnastics, dance, and music, certain decisions do have to made early). Well-planned and sensitive guidance and career counseling, as well as mentorships, can help students clarify their goals and directions over time.

"Why can't I do it this way?"

The creatively gifted student shares many qualities in common with the intellectually gifted student since a base level of intelligence is usually necessary for creative production. Characteristics of the creatively gifted include high energy, high motivation, risk taking, and complex personalities. Looked at from the other side, these qualities might be seen as impulsive and overactive, willingness to look or act foolish, asking unusual ("What if?") questions, or voicing nonconforming views—not always qualities that win classroom approval from peers or teachers. These students may prefer working alone and are often bored by routines. They enjoy finding ways to do things differently. Creatively gifted adolescents present unique challenges to their parents and teachers as they become increasingly independent and explore the "edges" of academics, the arts, and social roles.

Family/Home Relationships

Gifted children often have roles at home and in their families that have been defined by their precocity. As they enter adolescence, their relationships to their parents and their role within the family change. While this is true for all adolescents, several aspects of this development can be particularly unsettling for gifted students and their families.

For parents, their adolescent seems to have become a different person as he or she shifts from valuing intimacy with them to seeking intimacy with peers. Up until adolescence, many gifted children prefer the company of their parents and other adults to their peers because they find adult interests, conversations, and responses to their intelligence more valuable and rewarding. The pride and connection adolescents once took in spending time with their parents (and often their parents' friends) and sharing adult interests and pastimes may be limited or even ended. Parents may feel pushed away and disappointed, feeling they are, in some way, losing their child.

The adolescent need to explore alternatives, question, and test value systems can also lead to friendships that parents don't approve of. In addition, parents' expectations for their child's academic success are felt by the adolescent as pressure for perfection—"My parents think I have to have A's in everything" students have often reported to me. Parents have gained a great deal of satisfaction, and sometimes status, from their exceptional child, and as he or she seeks to find a peer group, parents feel they are losing the child or that the child is "not living up to his or her potential." Parents of gifted students have often been very involved and active in their children's elementary school lives, something children accepted with pride. But, in middle school, this can be an embarrassment for the student. Students who formerly enjoyed their many lessons and participation in outside clubs find that, during middle school, this takes away from being just a "normal" teen, and they may resent being "overscheduled" by their parents.

As the child with weak study skills confronts increasingly difficult material, parents may apply more pressure so that he or she doesn't "slip." They start to question the "gifted" label, and the child quickly senses parental disappointment. This additional external pressure is exactly what the child *does not* need. A student for whom school is too easy comes home with little or no homework, and parents are frustrated by the sudden turn to music, videogames, instant messaging with friends, and other typical adolescent activities.

Although it is sometimes difficult, parents need to let students relax and be themselves at home. When needed, they should help their children through difficult times, encourage talent exploration, help provide learning opportunities, and value their creativity and uniqueness (Schatz & Schuster, 1996).

So What?

Because of adolescents' unique social and emotional needs, all middle schools need to provide both cognitive and affective support services and programming for gifted students. These services should include specially trained teachers and counselors in every middle school. Parent education programs should complement the student services. In-service training should be provided for teachers to help them understand middle school gifted students and break down some of the stereotypes teachers often hold of how the gifted "should" behave and perform.

Intervention and support for students needs to be more than a 1-hour-per-week pull-out class. Students are gifted no matter what classroom they are in. A "range of services" model, similar to the planning used for special education students at the other end of the academic spectrum, should be used to plan appropriate educational opportunities for individual gifted students. Giftedness itself does not mean increased social and emotional vulnerabilities; rather, it is the mismatch between the student's personality, characteristics, cognitive style, and abilities and the educational environment that causes problems.

The key is to understand the complexities of middle school gifted students and design programming, instruction, and services based on their unique needs during this period of their development. In the following list, which reflects the range of academic and social/emotional concerns, students identified what *they* think schools should do in grades 5–8:

- encourage creativity;
- encourage independent learning;
- help smart kids not to feel alone;
- make academics equally as important as sports;
- eliminate the "nerd" attitude;
- respect students' learning abilities;
- push students to reach their limits; and
- allow students to learn at their own paces (Schatz & Schuster, 1996, p. 83).

Next Steps . . . Taking Action

1. Provide students with guidance and counseling, mentors, and role models who help them understand themselves better, including issues of multipotentiality, perfectionism, and difference.

2. Help students learn to deal with stress:
   - Say no.
   - Get exercise and practice good nutrition.
   - Take time out for relaxation and fun with supportive friends and family.

3. Watch out for unhealthy coping mechanisms and danger signals: eating disorders, overscheduling, drug and alcohol use, frequent illness, suicidal depression, or activity avoidance.

4. Create staff-development opportunities that help school personnel understand gifted adolescents during their middle school years.

5. Create procedures and plans that facilitate effective matching of gifted students with appropriate educational programs, courses, and materials. Offer a range of services to meet the needs of the various gifted, talented, high-achieving, and high-potential students.

6. Help gifted students find peer groups in which they are accepted and valued.

7. Help parents understand the changes their gifted children are experiencing as adolescents.

8. Encourage flexibility, resilience, and reasonable risk taking so that gifted students can learn and work comfortably in the middle school environment while striving to reach their potential. Help students create a balanced life of academics and other pleasures.

9. Teach gifted adolescents social skills that will help reduce the number of negative experiences they have in school.

10. Parents, teachers, and counselors need to communicate and work together on behalf of the students—mutual advocacy, rather than antagonism or competition.

References

Buescher, T. M. (1991). Gifted adolescents. In N. Colangelo & G. A. Davis (Eds.), *Handbook of gifted education* (pp. 382–401). Needham Heights, MA: Allyn and Bacon.

Buescher, T. M., & Higham, S. (2003). *Helping adolescents adjust to giftedness* (ERIC Digest #E489). Arlington, VA: The ERIC Clearinghouse on Disabilities and Gifted Education.

Clark, B. (2002). *Growing up gifted: Developing the potential of children at home and at school* (6th ed.). Upper Saddle River, NJ: Merrill/Prentice Hall.

Colangelo, N. (2004, October 18). *The road less traveled: Guiding students to choose rigorous curriculum.* Paper presented at the annual meeting of the Ohio Association for Gifted Children, Columbus.

Cross, T. L. (2004). *On the social and emotional lives of gifted children: Issues and factors in their psychological development* (2nd ed.). Waco, TX: Prufrock Press.

Dabrowski, K., & Piechowski, M. M. (1977). *Theory of levels of emotional development.* Oceanside, NY: Dabor Science.

Erb, T. O. (Ed.). (1997). *Dilemmas in talent development in the middle grades: Two views.* Columbus, OH: National Middle School Association.

Genshaft, J., & Broyles, J. (1991). Stress management with the gifted adolescent. In M. Bireley & J. Genshaft (Eds.), *Understanding the gifted adolescent: Educational, developmental, and multicultural issues* (pp. 76–87). New York: Teachers College Press.

Hébert, T. P. (2004). *Managing his image: The challenge facing a gifted male.* Retrieved April 12, 2005, from http://www.sengifted.org/articles_social/Hebert_ManagingHisImage.shtml.

Kaplan, L. S. (1990). *Helping gifted students with stress management* (ERIC Digest #E488). Arlington, VA: The ERIC Clearinghouse on Disabilities and Gifted Education.

Lind, S. (2001). Overexcitability and the gifted. *SENG Newsletter, 1*(1) 3–6.

Mendaglio, S. (2002). Understanding gifted children's emotions: Heightened multifaceted sensitivity. Retrieved April 12, 2005, from http://www.ucalgary.ca/~gifteduc/resources/articles/UnderstandingGiftedSM.pdf

Piechowski, M. M. (1986). The concept of developmental potential. *Roeper Review, 8,* 190–194.

Rakow, S. (1989, March). Gifted . . . and puberty too. *Middle School Journal, 20*(4), 18–19.

Robinson, N. M., Reis, S. M., Neihart, M., & Moon, S. M. (2002). Social and emotional issues facing gifted and talented students: What have we learned and what should we do now? In M. Neihart, S. M. Reis, N. M. Robinson, & S. Moon (Eds.), *The social and emotional development of gifted children: What do we know?* (pp. 267–288). Waco, TX: Prufrock Press.

Schatz, E., & Schuster, N. (1996). *Teens with talent: Developing the potential of the bright, brighter, and brightest.* Boulder, CO: Open Space Communications.

Schroeder-Davis, S. (1995). *Examining the climate for scholarship: Are our schools anti-intellectual?* Paper presented at annual meeting of the Ohio Association for Gifted Children, Cincinnati.

Sowell, T. (2000, May 7). In hoops or life, achievers deserve praise, not attack. *San Jose Mercury News.*

Additional Resources

Adderholdt-Elliott, M. (1991). Perfectionism and the gifted adolescent. In M. Bireley & J. Genshaft (Eds.), *Understanding the gifted adolescent: Educational, developmental, and multicultural issues* (pp. 65–75). New York: Teachers College Press.

Davis, G. A., & Rimm, S. B. (2004). *Education of the gifted and talented* (5th ed.). Boston, MA: Allyn and Bacon.

Delisle, J., & Galbraith, J. (2002). *When gifted kids don't have all the answers: How to meet their social and emotional needs.* Minneapolis, MN: Free Spirit.

DeLong, M. R., & Howell, W. C. (Eds.). (1995). *Full potential: A guide for parents of bright teens.* Durham, NC: TAG Books.

Galbraith, J., & Delisle, J. (1996). *The gifted kids' survival guide: A teen handbook.* Minneapolis, MN: Free Spirit.

Mendaglio, S. (2002, Fall). Dabrowski's theory of positive disintegration: Some implications for teachers of gifted students. *AGATE, 15*(2), 14–22.

Rimm, S. (2005). *Growing up too fast: The Rimm report on the secret world of America's middle schoolers*. New York: Rodale Press.

Silverman, L. K. (2000). Career counseling. In L. K. Silverman (Ed.), *Counseling the gifted and talented* (pp. 215–238). Denver, CO: Love.

National Reform Movements and Gifted Middle School Students

Essential Questions

1. What impact has the No Child Left Behind Act had on the middle school experiences and the achievements of gifted students?

2. What impact has *Turning Points 2000* had on the middle school experiences and achievements of gifted students?

3. How can middle schools implement the *Turning Points 2000* recommendations in ways that include meeting the needs of gifted students?

E very aspect of education and schooling in the past few decades has been influenced by national reports and statutes, from *A Nation At Risk* (U.S Commission on Excellence in Education, 1983) to the 2001 No Child Left Behind (NCLB) Act. The key goals of these were educational improvement through enhancing students' international competitiveness, development of measurable standards, and school accountability, all based on standardized test scores.

In middle school education, the Carnegie Council on Adolescent Development's 1989 report *Turning Points: Preparing American Youth for the 21st Century* brought the importance of middle schools to the nation's attention. More recently, the fol-

> "Democracy has been unjust to the gifted student."
>
> —John Dewey

low-up publication *Turning Points 2000: Educating Adolescents in the 21st Century* (Jackson & Davis, 2000) has continued efforts to implement these middle grades reforms. The combined impact of these forces on gifted education and gifted students has been devastating.

Leaving No Child Behind? What About the Gifted?

The No Child Left Behind Act's emphasis on competence, rather than excellence (i.e., "bringing up the bottom"), and its connection of school funding to the achievement of minimal standards have forced schools to focus all available resources on getting students to pass tests. Schools, districts, and even individual teachers may be evaluated based on the numbers of students who pass state and federally mandated proficiency tests.

Though the tests may vary by state, one result is the same: decreased attention to the needs of gifted students at every grade level. This is because the focus is on all students reaching a set standard, rather than maximizing everyone's individual potential. Gifted students may be the greatest victims of NCLB, making the lowest achievement gains and receiving the least funding (DeLacy, 2004). The absurdity of many of the aspects of NCLB is particularly apparent in the ways special education students are regarded, where NCLB is often in direct conflict with the Individuals With Disabilities Education Act (1990) and established Individualized Education Plans (Darling-Hammond, cited in Meier & Wood, 2004). Districts are required to spend huge sums of money on tests and testing; test preparation staff; and materials, data analysis, and reporting. The word *learning* has been replaced by *mastery, competence,* or *proficiency,* and many important social/emotional aspects of education have been lost.

My personal mentoring and staff-development experiences, as well as others' research (e.g., Popham, 2001) has revealed that classroom teachers are no longer teaching their best units and lessons. Though past students enjoyed and were engaged in these lessons and grew and learned as a result, the lessons were not connected directly enough to test items. All classroom activities must now demonstrate a specific proficiency outcome or, because of time constraints in the school day and year, face elimination in favor of test preparation. Coherent unit teaching with embedded standards has given way to "curriculum reductionism" (Popham, pp. 19–20)—individual, often disconnected, standards-based lessons.

In this environment, the school year becomes a series of classes preparing students for a particular test with a particular type of question—not a series of learning experiences designed to develop students' abilities, deep understanding, or love of learning.

> Simply put, with a focus on testing, the curriculum is narrowed, leading to the most ineffective teaching practices becoming the norm. As non-tested areas (art, music, social studies) and "frills" (field trips, naps, even recess) are eliminated, the school experience becomes limited, and everyone—children, parents, and communities— reports less satisfaction with the school. (Wood, cited in Meier & Wood, 2004, p. xii)

These are the aspects of schooling essential to the growth of all middle school students: broad and connected curricula, the arts, and studies that relate their own experiences and communities to the world at large and the solution of global problems. In addition, financial consequences of not meeting the federal standards penalize disadvantaged schools and children while rewarding the schools that were already successful.

When parents of gifted students feel that schools are no longer meeting their child's needs, they often have the economic resources to "escape" to private or charter schools, better-funded public schools in wealthier neighborhoods, or homeschooling. Gifted students whose families do not have such resources find themselves locked into a school whose lack of services results in underachievement and boredom.

The negative impacts of NCLB are reverberating throughout our educational system—but the loss of services to gifted children is particularly striking.

> To abide by the law, schools are shifting resources away from programs that help their most gifted students. Because "all the incentives in No Child Left Behind are to focus on the bottom or the middle," says Stanford University education professor Michael Kirst, "reallocating resources there makes sense if you want to stay out of trouble." (Golden, 2003, ¶ 4)

In Illinois, for example, $19 million for gifted education was deleted from the 2003 state budget. In the same year, California reduced funding for gifted education by $10 million (Golden). Currently, Javits grant support for research and initiatives in gifted education have been totally eliminated from the proposed federal budget.

One major urban Midwestern district reconfigured a previously award-winning gifted magnet middle school so that the students' high scores could be distributed throughout the district. It is now a heterogeneous K–8 building. In many other schools, ability grouping has been eliminated so that gifted students can help other students improve. The population of homeschooled children who are gifted is growing; parents feel public schools have turned their backs on them and cannot or will not meet their children's needs (Ensign, 1997, 2000; Kearney, 1992). While schools are bound by testing, curricula, grade levels, and so forth, parents who homeschool their gifted children can provide customization to individual needs, talents, and interests (Ray, 2002). In the schools' defense, some of their limitations are resource-related. Funds are limited and the federal and state governments have imposed the priorities districts must follow. Still, this is a tremendous loss that further separates gifted students from the democracy-building, pluralistic effects of public school.

Turning Points 2000: What About the Gifted?

Turning Points 2000 (Jackson & Davis, 2000), like its earlier edition, is used by middle school administrators and advocates as a set of "best practice" guidelines. Yet, in a movement dedicated to understanding the unique needs of early adolescents, this report ignores programs designed to meet the needs of gifted students and even denigrates them as being "a guise" (Jackson & Davis, p. 65). Naïve assumptions are made about teachers' abilities to accommodate the wide range of student abilities in today's heterogeneous classes, particularly in the No Child Left Behind era and with mandated inclusion of special education students.

The authors of this report, Anthony Jackson and Gayle Davis, are not teachers and have no direct recent experience with real-world classrooms or students. Their research (as indicated by their references) does not include any of the respected experts in the field of gifted education except Carol Tomlinson. Her work on differentiation seems to be the only tool Jackson and Davis support to both help teachers meet the needs of students in mixed-ability classrooms and fulfill their social justice agenda. Tomlinson's extensive work, as well as that of James Gallagher, Mary Ruth Coleman, Joseph Renzulli, Jim Delisle, Sally Reis, Tracy Cross, Laurence Coleman, myself, and others on middle grades/adolescent gifted students is ignored. Ability grouping is described solely as a tool of social segregation, racism, and injustice, rather than an option for meeting legitimate student needs— except as it pertains to special education where one-to-one tutoring and reading groups (such as The Reading Edge Program) are encouraged to bring students up to grade level. In addition, staffing of these remedial programs includes additional resource teachers, volunteers, and special training, again with the intention of ensuring that all students can perform *at* grade level, though not beyond. Jackson and Davis suggest that higher ability readers be used as tutors or be "allowed" to progress on their own to more sophisticated reading strategies (p. 91).

Comments in this report marginalize the concerns of parents of gifted students: "Parents of the students designated as 'gifted' often fear their children's education will be held back in untracked classes" (Jackson & Davis, 2000, p. 67). In fact, from what others and I have seen, their education *is* held back in such classes (Colangelo & Davis, 2003; Davidson, Davidson, & Vanderkam, 2004; DeLacy, 2004; Rogers, 2002). Criticism of teachers assigned to high- or low-ability-grouped classes, racial inequities in student identification and placement, and poor teaching strategies used in low-ability-grouped classes are not always invalid; however, even when valid, the elimination of ability grouping does not solve these problems. In fact, when gifted students flee public middle schools because their needs are not met, the schools become further segregated.

Efforts and Options

Tomlinson and George (2004) addressed some of these issues in their joint article "Teaching High Ability Learners in an Authentic Middle School." They reflected on the decade of conversation that has occurred between the two ideological "camps." Once again, however, the word *gifted* has been omitted in favor of the phrase "those whose academic performance exceeds grade expectations and those whose high potential is yet untapped" (p. 7). While perhaps more politically sensitive, it shows the tiptoeing necessary to try to bring the two sides together.

The same delicacy is evident in the October 2004 joint statement by the National Association for Gifted Children (NAGC) and the National Middle School Association (NMSA). Titled *Meeting the Needs of High Ability and High Potential Learners in the Middle Grades*, it presents a carefully worded set of general beliefs covering identification, assessment, curriculum and instruction, affective development, effective partnerships, and preservice/in-service staff development (see Appendix A). The adjective *gifted* is rarely used to describe students, preferring instead the term "high potential." The overall purpose of this document is to expand basic middle school philosophy to include "those with advanced performance or potential." The fact that such a statement was needed attests to the power of NMSA's previous neglect of gifted and talented students. Despite its tentative language, this report provides an important new beginning for dialogue, as well as action.

How Do We Know Who Has Advanced Abilities?

The question of identification was raised in *Turning Points 2000*, and several recent articles in *Roeper Review* have addressed the foundational concern of how to define giftedness.

Coleman (2004) took the position that a new consensus definition of giftedness similar to the one in the Marland Report (1972) might be helpful and more specific. However, he noted that, for the time being, the Marland definition is adequate:

Gifted and talented children are those identified by professionally qualified persons who, by virtue of outstanding abilities, are capable of high performance. These are children who require differentiated educational programs and/or services beyond those normally provided by the regular school program in order to realize their contribution to self and society. Children capable of high performance include those with demonstrated achievement and/or potential ability in any of the following areas, singly or in combination:

1. general intellectual ability
2. specific academic aptitude
3. creative or productive thinking
4. leadership ability
5. visual and performing arts
6. psychomotor ability. (p. 2)

Cramond (2004), however, disagreed, feeling that the "variety of definitions of giftedness that exists is necessary, to be expected, and beneficial" (p. 16). But, she also reminded us that there already is a federal definition from the U.S. Department of Education in the 1993 report *National Excellence: A Case for Developing America's Talent:*

> These children and youth exhibit high performance capability in intellectual, creative, and/or artistic areas, possess an unusual leadership capacity, or excel in specific academic fields. . . . They require services or activities not ordinarily provided by the schools. . . . Outstanding talents are present in children and youth from all cultural groups, across the economic strata, and in all areas of human endeavor. (p. 26)

In his article, Gagné (2004) also noted that a consensus is necessary, but concluded that

> while scholars continue to quarrel over the "true" nature of giftedness, most practitioners have operationalized that nature as "bright achievers." I wonder if my goal might be reached more easily and rapidly if the movement began with "real world" practitioners, then spread upwards to finally rally the thinkers in their ivory towers . . . (p. 14)

In addition to the federal definitions, individual states have developed their own definitions to guide the identification of gifted students. But, for people who are in the schools—Gagné's "real world practitioners"—the answer to the question of who the gifted students are is often obvious. There are multiple sources for this information: student classroom performance, standardized assessments, and content-specific preassessments. But, while these data sources are often used as the basis for providing remediation, they are rarely used to support the provision of accelerated opportunities. The information for solid decision making is already available in two of the three sources, but the third, preassessment, seldom occurs.

When middle school teachers are designing and developing engaging interdisciplinary units, a preassessment to find out what students already know is rarely part of the planning process. When it is used, it's usually just a K-W-L ("What do you *K*now?" "What do you *W*ant to know?" and "What have you *L*earned?") assessment on the first and last days of the unit.

Where, then, is the opportunity to plan thoughtfully and thoroughly for students who demonstrate that they already know most of the upcoming material or skills? Teachers offer the argument that even advanced students will benefit from the social interaction of standard lessons. However, social interaction without learning anything new is a poor use of gifted students' school time. They need both, just as typical students do: engaging activities with peers *and* learning. Students could go to camp if they wanted positive social interaction alone! Schools have a greater responsibility to provide both for all students, especially in middle schools with their emphasis on developmental responsiveness.

It is here that NCLB and the standards movement offer a tool for meeting the needs of gifted students: Use the standards and assessments to identify students who have already met the benchmarks. As Tomlinson and George (2004) suggested, "standards are the beginning of developing high quality curriculum, not the end" (p. 9). While these authors emphasize the need for balancing equity and excellence, practitioners should also consider the essential component of empathy (Rakow, 1994). All adolescents, including the gifted and talented, need educators who understand how they perceive the world, experience school, and feel about themselves in a middle school environment that often marginalizes them.

Renzulli and Reis (1997) support a move to label services students receive to develop gifted behaviors, rather than labeling students themselves as "gifted." While their goal, "the development of a total school enrichment program that benefits all students and concentrates on making schools places for talent development in young people," (p. 56) is laudable, this approach seems to deny the psychological, social, and emotional differences of giftedness that require significantly different school options.

To counteract the legacy of discrimination left by the single-IQ-measure approach to identifying gifted students, the standards movement has offered the untapped resource of multiple data sources. We have the opportunity to use these to find students who have already mastered grade-level standards and who both need and deserve appropriate advanced curricula and instructional services. Additionally, other approaches to examining student potential (learning style inventories, performance products, and portfolio evaluation) provide schools with opportunities to uncover students' abilities. Many new culture-fair assessments (e.g., the Naglieri Nonverbal Ability Test; Naglieri, 1997) help us identify gifted minority students who have been left out of these advanced opportunities for too long. It is this aspect of equity that needs to be embraced by gifted advocates while demanding that the "other side" pay more attention to the excellence issue.

How to Include Gifted Students and Meet the Turning Points 2000 Recommendations

There are seven *Turning Points 2000* recommendations, and each one can be implemented in ways that include and support gifted students, though the report itself never suggests that this is even a need or a goal to be considered. Horror stories abound among parents and teachers about how these recommendations have been used to defend ignoring gifted students and eliminating classes and curricula designed to serve them.

Rather than delineate the worst-case scenarios, let's examine instead what the best-case scenarios might look like. In each case, it's important to realize that implementation of any school or systemwide changes must balance issues of race, gender, and class equity, as well as the characteristics and circumstances of individual schools, districts, and communities. This is why these are not hard and fast rules, but rather guidelines to be considered when making decisions.

Recommendation #1: Teach a curriculum grounded in rigorous, public academic standards that is relevant to the concerns of adolescents and based on how students learn best.

Public academic standards, at the disciplinary level and the federal and state levels, can and should be part of any middle school's curricular planning process. *Turning Points 2000* recommends using a "backwards design" model for curriculum and instruction, starting with these standards, then selecting and creating appropriate assessments, and finally designing instruction. The report is appropriately critical of the "fun" or "cool" factor in creating classroom activities that are not clearly connected to any learning outcomes. The report states that "academic performance standards define excellence" (Jackson & Davis, p. 34). Unfortunately, this is not always true. Too frequently, the state and local standards being applied in schools and classrooms (fueled by NCLB) are minimum competency standards that are used as artificial ceilings for gifted students. Using the standards of professional organizations such as the National Council of Teachers of English (NCTE) or the National Council of Teachers of Mathematics (NCTM) might be more appropriate, consistent, and challenging, as well as less subject to local or regional politics.

The first key change that must be made is that teachers must assess what students know and can do, as well as how they learn, *before* specific lesson planning, grouping, and instruction begin. Ideally, administrators, counselors, teachers, and teaching teams should have general information at the end of the preceding school year. But, unit-specific or skill-specific preassessments should be part of the standard routine to identify areas of weakness for struggling students, as well as what has already been mastered by advanced students. Then, all curricular units should include accommodations for those who have already mastered the majority of the material, those who can master it quickly and need challenging extensions, and those who need remediation. The curriculum itself, regardless of grouping or students' entering abilities, should include higher level thinking, real-world applications, and challenging concept-based material for all students. Interdisciplinary and integrated units are cornerstones of good middle school curricula for all students. These also provide many opportunities for acceleration for gifted students and the kinds of curricular connections many gifted students need (Vars & Rakow, 1993).

The second key change that should be made is the use of above-grade-level standards in planning for gifted students. For example, the eighth-grade writing standards (which reflect greater depth and complexity in structure, syntax, vocabulary, etc.) might be used to guide instruction for advanced sixth- or seventh-grade students. In addition, the NAGC standards (see Landrum, Callahan, & Shaklee, 2001) that provide general guidelines for curriculum and instruction across content-areas should be included in designing advanced and accelerated opportunities for gifted students.

When considering the issue of relevance to adolescent concerns, it is important to realize that there is variation in what concerns subgroups of adolescents. The concerns of gifted students often differ significantly from their age peers (see Chapter 1), and they must be addressed just as there must be attention paid to the concerns of minority, bilingual, and special education students. The normal curve has *two* tails, not just the one on the left-hand side! For example, on *the very first day* of "Friday Forum," the advisory component of the middle school gifted program I designed and taught, one student asked to discuss the topic "What do you think happens to you when you die?" Another day, the topic of interest and concern were the comparative merits of Linux versus Microsoft operating systems and the impact on students' instant messaging and e-mail. These were not like any of the advisory group sessions I led with typical students over a 20-year middle school career! But, they *were* typical of many discussions with gifted students. In addition, the gifted students also wanted to discuss the usual adolescent concerns: inclusion/exclusion, school policies, movies, music, and so forth. Therefore, those who have experience with and understanding of gifted adolescents should be involved in middle school curriculum design and planning.

Recommendation #2: Use instructional methods designed to prepare all students to achieve higher standards and become life-long learners.

This should be the easiest to implement, yet it is a major stumbling block for gifted middle school students. Hands-on learning, for example, is one of the emphases in middle school because it can provide the bridge from the concrete example to the abstract concept. However, if students have already mastered the abstract concept, the concrete, hands-on work may be unnecessary. Many high-achieving students go through the motions of "Discovery Science" when they already know what it is they're supposed to be discovering. How many dioramas or terrariums does it take to understand the concept of ecosystem? To make matters worse, these hands-on learning activities are often done in supposed cooperative learning groups because of their potential for developing interpersonal relationships and social skills.

It's important to examine the application of cooperative learning a little more closely in light of this second recommendation. Cooperative learning is pervasive in middle schools because it can be an active and engaging strategy that is developmentally appropriate for typical middle school students. It usually allows for necessary social interaction and conversation, as well as physical movement. Students learning with and from each other supports constructivist philosophy.

But, cooperative learning is not just one strategy; it is a set of strategies, all of which share the common goal of having students work together to accomplish a common goal or receive a common reward (Robinson, 1991). Most of the models recommend heterogeneous ability or achievement grouping and include specific instructions for how to place high-, medium-, and low-achieving students in each group. Most models also include peer tutoring or partner teaching as a component and presume that all students are learning the same materials (Robinson). Some of these models are better for gifted students than others, and some can be applied effectively when student groups are made more homogeneous.

What does *Turning Points 2000* have to say about cooperative learning? In the chapter "Curriculum and Assessment to Improve Teaching and Learning" and in the section on disciplinary and interdisciplinary curriculum, cooperative learning's benefits seem to be as much about self-esteem and equality as curriculum and content: "Cooperative learning for example, can be a successful technique both to teach content to and raise self-esteem among all students, particularly those whose native language is not English" (Jackson & Davis, 2000, p. 48). In the chapter on "A Safe and Healthy School Environment," cooperative learning is applauded for its potential to develop interracial and intercultural relationships:

Cooperative learning and other project-based approaches to instruction are another way of improving student learning and promoting tolerance and understanding among different groups. Numerous studies show that cooperative learning groups promote cross-cultural friendships that are strong and long-lasting (from Slavin, 1995, p. 309) Cooperative learning groups seem to satisfy all the criteria identified in Gordon Allport's classic publication *The Nature of Prejudice* (1954) as needed to promote positive intergroup attitudes: equal status roles of students from different races, contact across racial lines that permits students to learn from one another as individuals, cooperation across racial lines, and communication by an authority figure of his or her unequivocal support for interracial (and intergroup) contact. (p. 176)

While these statements may be true, the research used to support it usually does not include gifted students and the impact cooperative learning has on them, especially in heterogeneous settings. Perhaps because teacher implementation of this approach does not always include the formal components prescribed by cooperative learning proponents and more likely resembles just cooperative group work, parents, students, and teachers frequently report frustration and dissatisfaction for gifted, talented, and advanced learners. When used in heterogeneous settings, cooperative-learning techniques rarely address the academic and learning needs of these students; rather, they are given the role as surrogate (or junior) teacher.

In 1993, the Gifted Education Policy Studies Program at the University of North Carolina, Chapel Hill, released a research report entitled *Cooperative Learning as Perceived by Educators of Gifted Students and Proponents of Cooperative Education* (Gallagher, Coleman, & Nelson). Their conclusions suggested that:

1. more preservice and in-service information must be provided for teachers to help them understand how to use this strategy appropriately with gifted students, including the

value of using the strategies in combination with ability grouping when appropriate;

2. the use of cooperative learning in classrooms should not be a reason for eliminating ability-grouped classes and other services for gifted students;

3. more work needs to be done to ensure that cooperative learning activities include adequate challenges for gifted students (Robinson [1991] found that, in most cases, cooperative learning studies defined achievement as basic skills outcomes); and

4. teachers should be aware of the potentially negative social and emotional consequences for all participants when gifted students act in the role of "junior teachers."

When cooperative-learning strategies are applied indiscriminately and without regard to the potential impact on gifted students, they may have exactly the opposite of their intended academic, social, or psychological effects. For example, while most students' academic self-concept increases in cooperative-learning groups, those very same students experience a significant decrease in social self-concept when they interact with gifted students.

Average ability children have more negative perceptions of each other when they are grouped with gifted students in cooperative groups. They view each other as less smart, less helpful, and less likely to be leaders than when they are grouped with other average ability students. (Siegle, 1994)

At the same time, many negative characteristics of gifted students such as arrogance and weak study habits are increased because they are too often the smartest person in the cooperative-learning group and the task isn't challenging enough to demand the advanced learning and study behaviors gifted students need to develop. Interdependence, a cornerstone of good cooperative learning, means that the contributions of all students are necessary for task completion. Often, the task is too narrowly defined, and gifted students can easily complete it without participation from any other group members. When grading procedures don't appropriately balance individual and group accountability, gifted students also find themselves "doing all the work" in order to earn a high grade, or they may be penalized for other students' lack of interest, motivation, ability, or shared definition of excellence.

So, in order to implement this recommendation in ways that meet the needs of gifted students, care needs to be given to what organizational structures, instructional approaches, and curricula will help (or, at minimum, not present obstacles to) this group of students becoming lifelong learners and achieving the highest standards of which *they* are capable. The following list of instructional approaches (which are described in greater detail in Chapters 3 and 4) can be used in both homogeneous and heterogeneous settings to benefit gifted students:

- the Autonomous Learner Model;
- Socratic seminars;
- independent and individualized study;
- simulations;
- creative problem-solving activities;
- Curry-Samara units based on the higher levels of Bloom's taxonomy;
- differentiated instruction that emphasizes depth, complexity, and advanced conceptual understanding in all content areas; and
- menu-model based on Bloom's taxonomy or Gardner's multiple intelligences to provide opportunities for student choice as well as advanced learning.

Recommendation #3: Staff middle schools with teachers who are expert at teaching young adolescents and engage teachers in ongoing, targeted professional-development opportunities.

Many states have revised their certification/licensure to include a middle grades (5–9) credential. Courses and field experiences are required that address the development and needs of middle grades students. Teacher-preparation programs also typically include courses in diversity and disabilities. Most of these courses, however, do not include substantive experiences and information on gifted students. Classroom field placements frequently include required experiences in remediation, tutoring, and diagnostic assessment; but, if preservice teachers are exposed to teaching and assessing gifted students, it is accidental, rather than intentional. Courses in assessment rarely include preassessment, authentic assessment of advanced performance, and aspects of testing that are particularly significant when examining the performance of gifted students (e.g., regression to the mean, out-of-level testing, and ceiling effects). For veteran teachers, their usual elementary (K–8) or secondary (7–12) licensure/certification programs also neglected specific preparation in the nature and needs of gifted students. Neither group is typically familiar with the limitations of standardized assessments for gifted students or the characteristics to look for in identifying them. However, a great deal of preservice and in-service time is spent on low-incidence disabilities, managing classroom behavior, and the indicators of higher incidence challenges such as ADD/ADHD, Asperger's Syndrome, autism, and dyslexia.

In most middle schools, teachers are given lists of students with IEPs or 504 plans during the earliest weeks of school. These delineate the accommodations they *must* legally make for these students. All too frequently, however, they are not given lists of students who have been identified as intellectually gifted or talented in a specific academic or creative arts area. Perhaps the assumption here is that these students will immediately make their unique abilities known to the teacher by outstanding achievement. Thus, there is no distinction made between gifted students and high-achieving "teacher pleasers": those who are neat, cooperative, prompt, and organized—who meet, but don't challenge or exceed teachers' expectations and requirements. This is a significant distinction in terms of meeting students' needs, particularly in the affective domain. In addition, the giftedness and potential of underachieving students (including many minority or twice-exceptional students) are often overlooked by classroom teachers.

This recommendation to ensure that teachers are expert at teaching young adolescents can be implemented in ways that respect and respond to gifted students in several ways:

1. Include a course in gifted education in preservice teacher preparation or, at the very least, a unit on gifted education in an existing diversity course. Additionally, any course in assessment should include assessment tools for gifted students (such as the various verbal and nonverbal intelligence tests, an Algebra Readiness Test, or the Iowa Acceleration Scale) and the limitations of standardized tests with gifted students (e.g., ceiling effects, out-of-level testing, regression toward the mean). Additionally, teachers should develop familiarity with interest and learning-style inventories that provide beneficial insights into all students.

2. Be sure that every middle school has a gifted education specialist in the building who is available to all teams in the same way that special education staff is allocated. Ideally, there would be one G/T resource teacher assigned to each grade-level team or, at the least, each grade level. This way, when teachers are planning interdisciplinary units, making grouping decisions, and selecting materials, someone is contributing the gifted perspective to the conversation, thus enriching the opportunities for all stu-

dents. The gifted specialist can help teachers design differentiated instruction for gifted students in the same way that learning-disabilities specialists help teachers modify curricula and instruction for learning-disabled students.

3. Middle schools should provide professional development in the area of gifted education—designing differentiated instruction, understanding the gifted adolescent, assessment and gifted students, flexible ability grouping, and acceleration—to fill in the gaps of preservice preparation programs. Often, district-level gifted coordinators or building-level gifted teachers can provide this or help arrange it.

Recommendation #4: Organize relationships for learning to create a climate of intellectual development and a caring community of shared educational purpose.

Teams (of teachers, as well as students) are the central component of good middle schools. They are designed to ensure collaboration among faculty so that no student "falls through the cracks" and so that curricula and instruction among teachers and subjects are aligned, coherent, and connected. Teaming is an organizational approach to understanding and meeting students' academic and affective needs. According to Mertens, Flowers, and Mulhall (1999), the single most important factor influencing student achievement is whether the school has interdisciplinary teams of teachers who plan and work together and share the same groups of students for a significant part of the school day.

Teaming, however, is often one of the roadblocks to meeting the needs of gifted middle school students. If there aren't enough students on a particular team to have a full class of, for example, sixth-grade Algebra, then the eligible students remain in "regular" sixth-grade math. This frequently occurs despite the fact that the advanced class would have enough students if it drew from the two or three teams at that grade level. The same applies to allocation of staff; for example, an eighth-grade team teacher could (if necessary) teach the sixth-grade advanced Algebra class to ensure high school credit and that the outcomes are consistent with what is taught to eighth-grade students taking the same course. Cross-teaming does not negate the positive effects of good teams; in fact, it can enhance them by manipulating schedules and staff assignments to ensure that *all* students are placed appropriately and have their needs met. Teaming and flexible use of ability grouping are not mutually exclusive.

One of the original and earliest middle school designs, the Lounsbury-Vars model, accommodated gifted and advanced students, as well as teaming and a curricular core that included advisory, social studies, English, and science. In this approach,

> subjects like math, foreign language, and reading were scheduled outside the core block so cross-graded competency-based instruction was facilitated as needed . . . having a skills block for all groups on teams at a particular grade level or in a particular pod makes it easier to use flexible ability grouping with fewer of the negative social side-effects. (G. Vars, personal communication, October 15, 2004)

It is common practice today to place the majority of special education students on one team in order to maximize the use of special-education faculty resources. For example, one team may have a cluster group of learning-disabled (LD) students so that the LD resource teacher can be on that team with her students, facilitating both inclusion and remedial self-contained learning opportunities. This approach, however, is rarely used for gifted students even though it would be equally effective. Instead, the gifted resource teachers (when they exist in a middle school) are usually "shared" by all the teams, and gifted students are spread out among them, thus diluting the resource teachers' impact on students and teachers and making student scheduling more difficult.

One administrative consideration when this is applied in gifted education is the community perception that there is a "smart" team and a "dumb" team. Sometimes, this can be mitigated by annually rotating which team has the LD resource teacher and students and which has the gifted resource teacher and students. In this way, all teams have the opportunity to learn from both specialists about how best to meet the needs of each unique group of students or of particular individual students.

Recommendation #5: Govern democratically through direct or representative participation by all school staff members, the adults who know the students best.

Another key element of middle schools advocated by *Turning Points 2000* is the leadership team. A gifted teacher/resource specialist should be included in this group to ensure a voice in the democratic leadership for gifted stakeholders. The resource teacher's participation in discussions about schoolwide events, curricular decisions, and student and parent conferences is important since he or she is frequently the adult who knows the gifted students best.

In most schools, special-education staff are part of the grade-level teaching teams because special-education and inclusion students are cluster-grouped on one particular team to ensure collaboration and communication in meeting the requirements of IEPs and 504 Plans. But, because there are fewer gifted staff and they often travel among buildings, they are rarely part of team meetings and team planning. If gifted resource staff rotate annually among the teams along with cluster-grouped gifted students, all teams will have the opportunity to work with gifted students and their resource teacher. Eventually, awareness and expertise in meeting the needs of gifted students will permeate all teams and benefit all students. This requires, however, taking a long-range view.

Recommendation #6: Provide a safe and healthy school environment as part of improving academic performance and developing caring and ethical citizens.

Bullying and anti-intellectualism in middle schools create a negative environment for gifted students. Communities often prefer "well-rounded" students over focused academic high achievers. Athletics is given far more media coverage and school attention than academics, and athletes are usually the most popular group, described by one scholar as the "governing elite" (Schroeder-Davis, 1995). Pep assemblies and sports banquets are often given much greater prominence than the honor roll assemblies, and students who receive academic honor certificates are rarely given the admiration of their sports counterparts. Middle schools may have an athletic director, but rarely an academic coordinator.

Peer pressure, particularly on girls and minority students, works against academic achievement. Complaints of bullying and harassment of "nerds" is not always taken seriously. Though this often changes in high school, middle school is a particularly painful time for many gifted students.

One potentially powerful solution to this problem is to use the advisory program, a cornerstone of model middle schools, to help create a supportive and healthy environment for gifted students. It can be a powerful time for gifted students to meet with the gifted teacher or counselor to help build the social and emotional survival skills necessary for middle school. In addition, heterogeneous advisory groups can address issues of academic achievement, bullying, and anti-intellectualism along with other issues of ethics and values.

Another solution is to create a school environment in which academic achievement and intelligence are honored and recognized through many of the same kinds of rewards that athletes receive. Students and the community-at-large need to realize that recognizing academic achievement is recognizing the same kind of hard work that leads to athletic success. It's not just heaping praise on students for an inborn quality like being blonde or tall.

The use of mentors for gifted students, especially minorities and girls, also helps them resist peer pressure to underachieve and provides support for challenging the narrow media images of success.

Recommendation #7: Involve parents and communities in supporting student learning and healthy development.

Parents of gifted students are also often left out of planning and decision making at the middle school level. Special-education parents who demand appropriate services for their children are seen as forceful advocates. On the other hand, gifted parents are seen as "pushy" and "elitist" when they request that their children's needs be met. Parents should be invited to be part of the principal's advisory councils, the parent-teacher association, and any district or regional organizations for parents of gifted students. Parents should also attend school board meetings and other district-level events where policy and organizational decisions are made that affect gifted students and their programming. Parents should not be made to feel embarrassed if they stand up and say, "I have a child who is gifted and this is what he or she needs." The role of parents here is critical because, especially in light of inadequate or no gifted services, they are often the adults who know the student best.

A districtwide group for parents of gifted students is also helpful in answering parents' questions. It can provide an opportunity to educate them about the school's gifted programs, other opportunities outside of school, and the nature and needs of their gifted adolescent. SENG (Supporting Emotional Needs of the Gifted) publishes a guide (Webb & DeVries, 1998) for starting and facilitating a support group for parents of gifted children (see http://www.sengifted.org/parents_groups.shtml).

Connecting Gifted Students to the Community

Turning Points 2000 lauds the value of after-school activities and programs as ways of connecting middle schools to the needs of the community. These provide opportunities for supporting gifted students, including programs such as Destination Imagination, drama club, chess club, MathCounts, and school newspapers or literary magazines. While they can and should be open to all students in the school (as sports teams are), they are especially beneficial to gifted students. Sometimes, parent volunteers can help coach these activities and the many competitions (like Knowledge Master Open) that appeal to gifted students. Additional information on these programs can be found in Chapter 9.

Another way of integrating gifted students into the community is through service learning, which also builds a sense of belonging and moral responsibility to others. Findings of a recent study (Terry, 2003) suggest that differentiated service learning can be an effective approach for gifted adolescents by involving them in activities based on individual interests and talents. Long-term service learning is especially beneficial, as activities that last longer than 18 weeks have been found to have a greater impact on student learning. Gifted students should certainly participate in school service projects with some attention to using problem-solving skills and ensuring adequate challenge, as well as social value. Students can have a direct positive impact on their community and be connected to real-world situations that lead to authentic learning.

Career Education for Gifted Students

Career education is especially important to gifted students whose multipotentiality often leaves them prey to the glib comment, "Oh, you can do anything you want." Career discussions in heterogeneous settings can be particularly painful for gifted students who may want to talk about what astrophysicists, ornithologists, or psychiatric social workers actually do or wonder what job they can have that will make a difference in the world, but find themselves limited to discussing the more narrow interests of typical adolescents. A variety of career education approaches are described in *Turning Points 2000*, including mentorships, career guidance and inventories, job shadowing, field trips, and project-based research on career fields. Jackson and Davis (2000) noted that "schools must ensure that the opportunities that are available are appropriate for a diverse population of students, including those with disabilities" (p. 213), and the same should apply to gifted students, with attention paid to their unique questions, concerns, and career directions. Teachers and counselors can also enhance the home-school connection for gifted students by providing information about community programs in the arts and content areas (such as those at local science and history museums or theaters), as well as summer and evening gifted programs and courses.

Next Steps . . . Taking Action

1. When considering the *Turning Points 2000* recommendations, ensure that implementation does not unfairly dismiss the concerns and needs of gifted students and their families.

2. Don't allow the minimum competencies established by the No Child Left Behind Act and state and local testing programs to limit gifted students' learning opportunities. Instead, use the standards of professional organizations or above-grade-level standards to guide decision making and student assessment.

3. Ensure that identification and placement are equitable and responsive to the needs of diverse gifted students.

References

Carnegie Council on Adolescent Development. (1989). *Turning points: Preparing American youth for the 21st century.* New York: Carnegie Corporation.

Colangelo, N., & Davis, G. A. (Eds.). (2003). *Handbook of gifted education* (3rd ed.). Boston: Allyn and Bacon.

Coleman, L. J. (2004) Is consensus on a definition in the field possible, desirable, necessary? *Roeper Review, 27,* 10–11.

Cramond, B. (2004). Can we, should we, need we agree on a definition of giftedness? *Roeper Review, 27,* 15–16.

Davidson, J., Davidson, B., & Vanderkam, L. (2004). *Genius denied: How to stop wasting our brightest young minds.* New York: Simon and Shuster.

DeLacy, M. (2004, June 23). The "No Child" law's biggest victims? An answer that may surprise. *Education Week, 23*(41), 40.

Ensign, J. (1997). *Homeschooling gifted students: An introductory guide for parents* (ERIC EC Digest #E543). Arlington, VA: The ERIC Clearinghouse on Disabilities and Gifted Education. Retrieved May 4, 2005, from http://www.hoagiesgifted.org/eric/e543.html

Ensign, J. (2000) Defying the stereotypes of special education: Home school students. *Peabody Journal of Education, 75,* 147–158.

Gagné, F. (2004). An imperative, but, alas, improbable consensus. *Roeper Review, 27,* 12–14.

Gallagher, J., Coleman, M. R., & Nelson, S. (1993). *Cooperative learning as perceived by educators of gifted students and proponents of cooperative education.* Chapel Hill: Gifted Education Policy Studies Program, University of North Carolina. (ERIC Document Reproduction Service No. ED 355675)

Golden, D. (2003, December 29). Initiative to leave no child behind leaves out gifted. *Wall Street Journal.* Retrieved May 5, 2005, from http://online.wsj.com/public/resources/documents/Polk_Gifted.htm

Individuals With Disabilities Education Act, 20 U.S.C. §1401 (1990).

Jackson, A. W., & Davis, G. A. (2000). *Turning points 2000: Educating adolescents in the 21st century.* New York: Teachers College Press.

Kearney, K. (1992). Homeschooling highly gifted children. *Understanding Our Gifted, 5*(1), 16. Retrieved May 6, 2005, from http://www.hollingworth.org/HomSchHG.html

Landrum, M. S., Callahan, C. M., & Shaklee, B. D. (Eds.). (2001). *Aiming for excellence: Annotations to the NAGC pre-K–grade 12 gifted program standards.* Waco, TX: Prufrock Press.

Marland, S. P., Jr. (1972). *Education of the gifted and talented: Report to the Congress of the United States by the U.S. Commissioner of Education and background papers submitted to the U.S. Office of Education,* 2 vols. Washington, DC: U.S. Government Printing Office. (Government Documents, Y4.L 11/2: G36)

Mertens, S. B., Flowers, N., & Mulhall, P. (1999, Winter). Teaming up for higher test scores. *Middle Matters, 5,* 7.

Meier, D., & Wood, G. (Eds.). (2004). *Many children left behind: How the No Child Left Behind Act is damaging our children and our schools.* Boston: Beacon Press.

Naglieri, J. A. (1997). *Naglieri nonverbal ability test.* San Antonio, TX: The Psychological Corporation.

National Association for Gifted Children & National Middle School Association. (2004). *Meeting the needs of high ability and high potential learners in the middle grades: A joint position statement of the National Association for Gifted Children (NAGC) and the National Middle School Association (NMSA).* Retrieved May 5, 2005, from http://www.nagc.org/middleschools/index.html

No Child Left Behind Act, 20 U.S.C. §6301 (2001).

Popham, W. J. (2001). *The truth about testing: An educator's call to action.* Alexandria, VA: Association for Supervision and Curriculum Development.

Rakow, S. (1994). *Excellence, equity, and empathy: The dilemma of educating the gifted adolescent in the middle school.* Unpublished doctoral dissertation, Kent State University, Kent, OH.

Ray, B. D. (2002). Customization through homeschooling. *Educational Leadership, 59*(7), 50–54.

Renzulli, J. S., & Reis, S. M. (1997). Giftedness in middle school students: A talent development perspective. In T. O. Erb (Ed.), *Dilemmas in talent development in the middle grades: Two views* (pp. 43–112). Columbus, OH: National Middle School Association.

Robinson, A. (1991). *Cooperative learning and the academically talented student* (Report No. 9106). Storrs: National Research Center on the Gifted and Talented, University of Connecticut.

Rogers, K. B. (2002). *Re-forming gifted education: How parents and teachers can match the program to the child.* Scottsdale, AZ: Great Potential Press.

Schroeder-Davis, S. (1995). *Examining the climate for scholarship: Are our schools anti-intellectual?* Paper presented at the annual meeting of the Ohio Association for Gifted Children, Columbus, OH.

Siegle, D. (Ed.). (1994). *What educators need to know about gifted students and . . . cooperative learning.* Storrs: National Research Center on the Gifted and Talented, University of Connecticut.

Terry, A. W. (2003). Effects of service learning on young, gifted adolescents and their community. *Gifted Child Quarterly, 47,* 295–308

Tomlinson, C. A., & George, P. S. (2004). Teaching high ability learners in an authentic middle school. *Middle School Journal, 35*(5), 7–11.

U.S. Commission on Excellence in Education. (1983). *A nation at risk: The imperative for educational reform.* Washington, DC: U.S. Government Printing Office.

U.S. Department of Education, Office of Educational Research and Improvement. (1993). *National excellence: A case for developing America's talent.* Washington, DC: U.S. Government Printing Office.

Vars, G. F., & Rakow, S. R. (1993). Making connections: Integrative curriculum and the gifted student. *Roeper Review, 16,* 48–53.

Webb, J. T., & DeVries, A. R. (1998). *Gifted parent groups: The SENG model.* Scottsdale, AZ: Great Potential Press.

Organizational Structures and Program Models: Developing a Continuum of Services

Essential Questions

1. What are the options for effective organizational structures through which gifted students can be served in middle school?

2. How do individual schools and districts decide among the available options?

3. How do we ensure that our choices support excellence *and* equity?

The 2003 National Middle School Association's position statement on middle level education, *This We Believe*, describes what a successful school for young adolescents includes in its culture and what it provides for its students. The document describes the school itself as place in which students learn not only in the classroom, but also from the ways adults with a shared vision treat each other and make decisions. These schools are inviting, supportive, and safe places where every student has an adult advocate who knows him or her well. The curriculum in these schools is relevant, challenging, integrative, and exploratory, and instruction draws on multiple learning and teaching approaches that are responsive to student diversity.

Organizational structures are developed that support meaningful relationships and create learning communities where all students and teachers are actively engaged. "The interdisciplinary team is the signature component of high-performing schools, literally the heart of the school." (National Middle School Association, p. 29). These teams range from two to four teachers and can include either multiple or (more commonly) single grade levels. Common planning time is provided for these teams to integrate curricula and share information about students. Sometimes, these teams of teachers and students are looped together for several years. NMSA recommends scheduling a block of time for core subjects that allows for extended learning activities and remedial or enrichment opportunities. Other elements of an exemplary schedule include advisory programs and exploratory courses like art, music, foreign language, and computer, as well as health and physical education.

This selective summary portrays an ideal environment for gifted and talented, as well as typical, middle school students. But, there is a significant gap between theory and practice here as in many areas of education. Even the grade levels (usually some combination of fifth through ninth) included in a given middle school are dependent upon a school district's population, demographics, facilities, and needs, rather than what's best for early adolescents. Teams may be established without adequate materials and curricula to meet the needs of their range of students and sometimes even without the common planning time that is essential to effective functioning and critical interdisciplinary unit design and development. Teams may be strongly affected by special education students' requirements and accommodations, as well as demands of standardized testing. Schedules become based on staff shared with other schools or "singletons" (i.e., only one period of band or Latin) and thus become inflexible. Teachers are assigned advisory groups with little preparation or guidance (especially with respect to the needs of gifted and talented students), and group time becomes a vehicle for recordkeeping, student council, school spirit activities, or study hall, rather than relationship building, guidance, and student advocacy. Some administrators interpret documents like *Turning Points 2000* (see Chapter 2) as "musts," rather than explorations of directions and ideas. George (1997) noted that

> the most desirable components of the middle school concept are not always part of the daily experiences of the gifted young adolescent students. . . . [I]n their commitment to the success of all students, some middle school educators have created circumstances where advocates of the gifted have a right to be concerned. Some middle school programs may, for example, develop an imbalance that overemphasizes the affective domain at the expense of the cognitive. Gifted students' intellectual needs may, indeed, sometimes suffer during the middle school years if at least equal attention is not given to both the mental and the social-emotional needs of students. (p. 114)

So, rather than becoming an ideal setting for gifted students, middle schools can become something to be endured—time spent, at best, treading academic water.

Because of the variations in middle school structure and organization, there is no "best" way to organize and coordinate services for gifted students. No one perfect model can be "dropped" into a particular school to guarantee success. There are, however, a variety of programming models and options that middle schools can use to serve their gifted students while still striving to incorporate the core elements of middle school philosophy and practice. The goal is to design services so that they are a good "fit" for the overall context. In addition, as with any other group of special-needs students, a school or district should provide a continuum or range of services in order to meet the varying needs of individual gifted students, from an independent study project, to placement in a general education classroom with differentiated assignments. The choices will depend on (a) the student population overall, (b) the identified students themselves, (c) the community, (d) the size of the school and the district, (e) the location (rural, urban, suburban), (f) the structure of the school, (g) available resources (materials and human), (h) existing opportunities, and most significantly, (i) the commitment and will of the district and school to meet gifted students' needs. Each design has its pros and cons, and some are more appropriate to particular settings than others. Additionally, various elements can be combined; in fact, in most cases, aspects of various models *should* be combined to avoid the negative effects of tracking.

One of the earliest examinations of program structures was *Middle School Site Visit Report: Five Schools in Profile* (Coleman, Gallagher, & Howard, 1993). The purpose of this study was to examine schools that had successfully combined both effective services for gifted students and model programming for middle schools. This study found that it was definitely possible to blend "appropriately differentiated services for gifted students into schools operating within an authentic middle school paradigm . . . approaches can be highly individualized and still lead to successful collaboration" (Coleman et al., p. v). The key elements that contributed to this success were (a) autonomy of principals and teachers, (b) school site administration, (c) availability of expertise and human resources, (d) enthusiasm of students and teachers, (e) a sense of trust and commitment to the school, and (f) curricular differentiation that used some form of instructional (ability/performance) grouping and enrichment.

The study also looked at the service-delivery models in each of the five schools. The one common element was ability-grouped math and language arts classes in all schools. Other structural elements varied and included rotating daily pull-out classes, a gifted class taught during a school enrichment period when *all* students participated in some type of enrichment class, a separate gifted class (2 schools), and cluster grouping of gifted students on a single team (3 schools). Thus, all five schools seemed to combine several approaches in order to be successful and adequately meet gifted students' needs.

In 1992, I surveyed 611 middle schools throughout the state of Ohio (Rakow, 1994). I also identified and did case studies of three schools that reflected different approaches to offering successful and rewarding opportunities for gifted students while still retaining middle school philosophy and practices. In these three schools, certain attitudes seemed to exist that set them apart from schools that were less successful in accommodating the needs of gifted and talented students:

1. *Advocacy and commitment.* Someone in the school system (parent, gifted teacher, administrator) pushed the school forward. This individual had strong faith in gifted programming and gifted students and in their value to the school and system. This individual provided a committed and constant voice on students' behalf.

2. *Flexibility.* At every school site, flexibility was mentioned as part of their success. This included flexible approaches to scheduling, students, faculty, philosophy, or new ideas. People were willing to compromise, and schools were willing to adjust to change and innovation. The school wasn't dogmatic or limited in the way it interpreted and applied middle school philosophy. This flexibility was also related to the autonomy of principals and teachers and their empowerment to make necessary changes without excessive bureaucratic interference.

3. *Practicality.* Successful schools and programs were practical. They addressed questions such as "What will work *here*?," "What do we already have?," and "What will our community, our building, our principal, accept?" Staffing selections were made after thoughtful assessment of existing teachers' strengths. Being practical and pragmatic also meant that no single constituency got everything it

wanted or even exactly what it wanted. The key was that everybody tried to come close to an ideal.

Of the three models, one was a magnet school for both cognitively and artistically gifted students in grades 4–8. The second was in the process of evolving from a junior high to a middle school. Gifted students in grades 4–7 spent 1 day a week in a resource room off-site, while accelerated courses were provided for them on-site in grade 8 (math, foreign language, English/language arts). The third school based its gifted program in advanced English classes and additionally conducted a seminar program.

Thus, both studies offer examples from which we can confidently conclude that combining effective and appropriate elements of middle school and gifted education is possible in a variety of settings. The possibilities described below provide a menu of options from which individual schools can create a continuum of services for gifted students that fits into their overall setting.

Magnet Middle Schools

Magnet schools for the gifted are most often used in large urban districts. They are separate schools with specific criteria for identification of giftedness and admission. They often include a wider age range than just middle school, either combining with elementary grades or with high school. Some magnet schools may also include a focus on the arts.

The advantages of magnet schools begin with the fact that they are staffed with specially trained teachers, counselors, and administrators. They share the common goal of providing appropriately challenging curricula and instruction for gifted students. They also understand the social and emotional needs of their students. Magnet schools also offer a built-in peer group for students. Even profoundly gifted students may find others they can relate to and befriend.

Students are served all day, not just a few hours a week or a period or two a day. While scheduling is a common reason given for why services cannot be provided for gifted students in a typical middle school, magnet schools are scheduled specifically to serve their unique population. Students may still have to make compromises in order to take all the courses at their level or that interest them; but overall, the schedule itself is designed around gifted students.

Magnet schools for gifted students can still incorporate all of the essential elements of model middle schools (interdisciplinary teams and curricula, advisory programs, etc.) and can ensure safe and healthy environments. Thus, despite their focus on a particular group of students, they can provide developmentally appropriate instruction.

But, this model is not perfect. Though the instructional model is cost-effective, transportation of students may be costly. At the high school level (such as in Indiana and North Carolina), magnet schools are boarding schools and students live on site. But, middle school students are too young for this, so parents must provide transportation, students must use public transportation, or the school district must provide transportation. Unlike other areas of special education, transportation is not usually covered by federal dollars.

The establishment of a magnet school for gifted students may have negative effects on the rest of the district. Students' high test scores may not be recorded for their neighborhood schools and, as a result of the No Child Left Behind Act, funding for other schools may suffer. There are also implications for sports team membership, as students may want to participate in their neighborhood school programs. Another problem exists with identification and placement. Students may not be gifted in all areas and therefore may struggle in a school where every class is designed for those who are gifted. Additionally, without careful selection, testing and assessment instruments may not encourage diverse racial and ethnic representation. It may also be harder to meet the needs of twice-exceptional (e.g., gifted/LD, gifted/handicapped, gifted/ADD, etc.) students since the magnet school may lack necessary special education support services.

One last interesting consequence in some magnet schools exists for those students at the "bottom" of the talent pool. These students, though in the top 10% or higher of the overall population, may feel "dumb" in a magnet school full of other gifted students. So, the question for each student is the big fish/little pond, little fish/big pond dilemma. Facilities, too, may create disparities. The magnet school may have superior arts or technology facilities that further separate those who are already advantaged from those whose schools lacked such resources. It would be important to ensure that the per-pupil expenditures are consistent and equitable throughout a district.

School Within a School

In a large middle school or district, the school-within-a-school model may be an appropriate choice. In this model, a wing or a clustered group of classrooms within a building along with a specific group of specially trained teachers, counselors, and administrators (depending on the size) are provided to serve gifted students. Multiple grade levels are included to reflect the grade-level make-up of the whole school.

There are several advantages. It is cost-effective and provides full-day services. Students have the advantages of interacting with typical students at lunch, in unified arts areas, and on sports and academic teams. At the same time, they have a peer group of other gifted students with whom they can feel comfortable. This approach can be part of all the middle schools in a district or just in several that are geographically spread out to provide accessibility for all qualified students. Students can move in and out of the program as needed for other support services or electives. Students' test scores can still contribute to those of the whole school. Facilities would be those of the whole school, thus equity in resource allocation would not be an issue.

The disadvantages are similar to those of a magnet school. Identification and placement criteria must be clear and sensitive to the student population, working toward equity and appropriate representation of minority and twice-exceptional students. If this is not done, racial and ethnic isolation may result. It is also important to look at class sizes to ensure that gifted students' classes are not consistently smaller in all areas than those of typical and other special-education students in the same building. In some cases, this can't be avoided, as for example, if just a handful of eighth graders are ready for Honors Algebra II, having already completed Honors Algebra I and Honors Geometry. If there are not enough gifted students in a single school to ensure that these questions of equity are addressed, perhaps another approach (maybe regional) is necessary.

Homogeneous Gifted Teams or Gifted Clusters

In some middle schools, it may be possible to have a homogeneous gifted or honors team, either multigrade or at each grade level. This is best when the school is large enough to have three or more teams at each grade level. The gifted team can be staffed by a combination of secondary and middle school certified people to ensure enough content depth and understanding to provide appropriate instruction for advanced students. In addition, teachers should have (or be provided with) special training in meeting the needs of gifted students. A gifted resource specialist should also be part of the team. Students on the gifted team may have unified arts, gym, music, and lunch periods with the rest of the student body and may participate in whole-school activities such as sports, drama, and the school newspaper. This allows for a balance of homogeneous and heterogeneous social experiences while advanced academic needs are met.

One advantage of this model is that students are more integrated into the school as a whole. Also, teachers are skilled and knowledgeable, and the team is focused on the needs of gifted students. Services are provided throughout most of the student's day. When multigrade teams are constructed, students have a broader group of gifted peers. Again, this is cost-effective if enough identified students are in a school, since the students would have to be on a team anyway.

The challenge of this model is in the potential community perception that there's a "smart" team where the "best" kids and teachers are and where there are no behavior problems. This perception must be challenged by administrators and teachers who provide top-notch instruction, materials, activities, and personnel on *all* teams. When all students are achieving and progressing and all students' needs are met by their team placement, this rivalry does not have to be a problem.

It is also important that the gifted team be racially and ethnically reflective of the total school population; thus, identification and placement tools must be culturally responsive and appropriate. The gifted team should not and cannot be a tool of racial segregation while it strives to meet the academic and social needs of gifted students. The twin goals of equity and excellence must be constantly kept in view. Though these may be difficult to achieve, especially during a time when schools are working so hard to close the minority student achievement gap, every effort must be made to identify gifted minority students. In the best of all possible worlds, this gap would not exist and, therefore, gifted teams and classes would reflect the racial makeup of the community's population. In the meantime, disproportionate minority representation should not be used as an excuse for failing to provide services for gifted students because otherwise both minority and majority gifted students suffer.

A more common variation on this approach is a gifted cluster on one team. This is usually the way special-education students are grouped; they are placed on a particular team along with a special-education resource or intervention teacher. Identified gifted students (usually only those identified as superior cognitive gifted, but sometimes those identified in math or reading/language arts, as well) are placed on a particular team with teachers who are required to have additional expertise in meeting the needs of such students.

When cluster groups are used, it is also recommended that the most severely disabled students (learning or physically) not be placed on this team because it puts an inequitable burden on the teachers and widens the performance gap beyond what most teachers can reasonably be expected to address. In addition, cluster-grouping gifted students on a team should not substitute for having ability-grouped classes. It is an organizational structure best used in combination with other programming (e.g., ability-grouped classes, pull-out enrichment, homogeneous gifted advisories, subject-area acceleration). The advantages of a gifted peer group, however, are retained in a gifted cluster while at the same time providing other opportunities for students to interact with a range of diverse students.

Whether it is best to have a totally homogeneous gifted team or to cluster group gifted students on one team is often dependent on school and team size, as well as available human and material resources.

Homogeneous Gifted/Honors Classes

In research studies of how middle schools meet the needs of gifted students, the most common service provided is ability-grouped math and language arts/reading classes (Rakow, 1994; Rogers, 1991). If classes are blocked to enhance interdisciplinary connections (in math/science or language arts/social studies), then gifted students gain the benefit of the double-period honors curriculum. Some schools also have separate honors, accelerated, or pre-AP/IB classes in social studies and science, but this is much less common.

Most middle schools offer foreign language to all students, while others make it available only to high-achieving and gifted students. Some schools provide 2 years of foreign language (grades 7 and 8), which equal first-year high school language. Others provide the accelerated opportunity for high-ability students to complete 2 years of foreign language during middle school, entering high school at the third-year level.

For most honors classes, student placement is based on a content-specific assessment, gifted identification criteria, or a nationally normed test in combination with other factors (e.g., teacher recommendations, parent recommendations, grades, demonstrated performance). The clearer the placement criteria, the less parental pressure there is to place students in a class that may be beyond their reach. Alternatively, these criteria should not be used to deny this opportunity to underachieving high-potential minority students. So, there must also be flexibility. This is a delicate balance.

Students may be enrolled in one or all available honors options depending on their abilities and potential. Ideally, each grade-level team will have a section of any available honors classes. Occasionally, when enrollment is low, there will be one class (e.g., Honors Algebra in grade 7) in which identified and advanced students from all teams participate.

The advantage of honors classes is that students' needs for accelerated and advanced curricula and experiences are met in their particular area of talent. These classes are taught by content experts with understanding of how to accelerate material and take it to deeper and more complex levels. Another advantage is that students with a strong ability in just one subject are provided with advanced instruction in that area without having to qualify for placement using more stringent superior cognitive (IQ or ability) gifted identification criteria. A final advantage is that, when pre-AP (College Board Advanced Placement) or pre-IB (International Baccalaureate) curricula are used in middle school, articulation with high school AP and IB programs is improved. Students will then have a better chance of successfully completing these courses because they will be prepared for their rigor and demanding academic expectations.

The disadvantage is that this is not necessarily gifted education. Gifted students still need their unique social and emotional needs met, something honors class teachers, who are usually secondary-certified content specialists, aren't qualified to do. Another disadvantage occurs when ability grouping for two classes leads to a student's whole day becoming "tracked" because of scheduling limitations. In a small school, once a student is in, for example, advanced math, advanced reading, foreign language, and band, his or her schedule may become fixed, and he or she may move with the same small group throughout the whole day.

One alternative is to schedule or "house" the superior cognitive gifted program in a particular subject class, the most common of which is English/language arts. Identified superior cognitive gifted students are scheduled in a gifted English class where the content is compacted and accelerated and room is made in the curriculum for other areas necessary for gifted students: problem solving, independent research skills, career education, and social and emotional development. This avoids many of the problems created by pull-out programs (discussed later in this chapter).

The research on ability grouping is politically charged and often mixed with dogmatic antitracking stances. There is a difference between tracking (which is more permanent and inflexible) and ability grouping (which is more flexible and responsive to students' changing development and needs). The research on ability grouping for the gifted (Fiedler, Lange, & Winebrenner, 1993; Kulik & Kulik, 1992; Rogers, 1991, 1998; Renzulli, 1977; VanTassel-Baska, n.d.) supports this practice as valuable when combined with changes in curricular and instructional goals. Rogers' (1991) review of the research revealed "consistent support for the academic effects of most forms of ability grouping for enrichment and acceleration" (¶ 3). Slavin (1986) recommended that students be placed primarily in heterogeneous classes, with regrouping by ability only in subjects such as reading and math where reducing heterogeneity is particularly important. There must be frequent reassessment and flexible reassignment, and teachers must actually vary their level and pace of instruction to meet students' needs in regrouped classes. Messick and Reynolds (1992) suggested that Slavin's elements of effective grouping plans for elementary students can apply to early adolescents, as well.

The research on ability grouping for struggling and low-ability students is generally negative. Offering several ability-grouped subject classes and several heterogeneously grouped classes is often the trade-off districts and principals make in order to avoid the negative effects of tracking for the lower ability students, especially in small schools. The cost of the trade-off, however, is born by the gifted student unless teachers make serious and consistent efforts to differentiate instruction appropriately in the heterogeneous general education classroom.

The Schoolwide Enrichment Model

The Schoolwide Enrichment Model (SEM; Renzulli & Reis, n.d.) has been revised, expanded, and developed in many ways since its origination in the Enrichment Triad Model (Renzulli, 1977). However, the intention of the model has remained to develop a broad range of students' talents and enhance curricula and opportunities for all students in a school community. It is a schoolwide reform model designed to fit within a school's existing organizational structure. It aims to revitalize the overall educational environment, create engaged and independent learners, and provide a higher level and quality of learning experiences for students capable of high levels of performance. The SEM is based on a broad conception of giftedness and talent that differentiates between "schoolhouse" and "creative productive" giftedness, including Renzulli's Three-Ring Conception of Giftedness: task commitment, creativity, and academic achievement.

The SEM has multiple interrelated components. The starting point is the Total Talent Portfolio (TTP), an individual portrait of a student's abilities, interests, and style preferences. This provides the basis for educational decision making that matches each student with appropriate options from the special services continuum. The Enrichment Triad Model (ETM) forms the core of the enrichment component of the SEM. It is based on three levels of activities:

- Type I Enrichment provides introductory and general exploratory activities. Students are exposed to new topics, ideas, and interests through guest speakers, various media, and whole-class or school presentations. These activities are usually teacher-directed.
- Type II Enrichment, usually for smaller groups of students who demonstrate interest, provides a deeper level of instruction and involvement with the topic. Students develop higher level thinking processes and research skills.
- In Type III Enrichment, individual students become "experts" and extend their research studies into real-world problems, becoming producers, rather than consumers, of knowledge. Creative products are developed and shared with authentic audiences. Students often engage in apprenticeships, mentorships, and competitions.

In many cases, the Type II and Type III activities are provided or supported by the gifted intervention specialist, who either partners with the general education teacher in his or her classroom or works with students in a pull-out setting.

The second complementary service-delivery component of the SEM involves a series of curricular modification techniques such as curriculum compacting, subject or grade acceleration, within-grade-level and across-grade-level advanced classes, mentorships, and cocurricular competitions and clubs.

Enrichment clusters comprise the third service-delivery component of the SEM. These consist of nongraded groups of students who come together weekly to explore a common interest under the guidance of an adult who shares the interest and who has additional expertise and knowledge of the topic.

The Schoolwide Enrichment Model has often been praised by middle school advocates like Paul George, but it has been applied only selectively. The emphasis has been placed on schoolwide enrichment and heterogeneous opportunities without the use of the TTP or the other curricular modifications. In some cases, implementation of selected components of the SEM has been used to justify eliminating ability-grouped classes and gifted intervention specialists. In an article on their Web site (http://www.sp.uconn.edu/~nrcgt/sem/whatisem.html), Renzulli and Reis addressed many of the concerns of gifted advocates, including a redesigned continuum of services that includes ability-grouped classes and the essential component of a gifted intervention specialist in each building. When implemented with *all* of its interconnected parts, this model has great potential to blend the goals of both middle school and gifted education. The Academies of Inquiry and Talent Development (described in Chapter 5) that evolved from the SEM are specifically designed for middle schools.

Pull-Out Resource Programs and Gifted Advisory

A variety of models exist that pull gifted students out of their regular classrooms in order to receive gifted services. Sometimes, students are transported to a different location where they spend a whole or half day a week engaging in enrichment projects, independent study, seminars, and field trips provided by specially trained gifted resource teachers or mentors. Another model pulls students out of a heterogeneous class one or more periods a week in their area of ability or talent; for example, identified gifted math students may leave the math classroom one or two periods a week to do problem solving or other advanced activities in the gifted resource room. Another model pulls students out one period a day to the gifted resource room, rotating the period each day to minimize the classwork missed. Thus, students are out of each class about once every 2 weeks. This allows the gifted teacher to have continuity and do unit teaching in nontraditional areas such as medical inventions or architecture or focus on themes such as identity or interpersonal communication skills.

The disadvantages of this model are related to classroom teachers and to this stage of middle school students' social-emotional development. Particularly in the era of No Child Left Behind, classroom teachers feel especially accountable for the material they cover during class. So, gifted students who leave for pull-out services are often forced to make up classwork and homework. Some teachers resent having students leave their rooms and, rather than use the time to review with less-capable students or reinforce already learned material with students who need it, they do games or deliberately introduce new information. This kind of sabotage may seem petty and mean-spirited, but it occurs more frequently than many schools are willing to admit. Just ask gifted kids, many of whom drop out of gifted programs for this reason. Because most gifted students are high achievers who are dedicated to getting A's, as well as to learning, they are unwilling to do double work or to risk missing assignments (and therefore losing points) by participating in the pull-out program. Some school districts have found it useful (in fact, necessary) to create policies about make-up work when students are attending the gifted pull-out. It is important, though, to delineate faculty responsibility for grading and for standardized testing when a pull-out structure is used.

The second major drawback is developmental. Middle school gifted students, as opposed to their elementary school counterparts, are often embarrassed by pull-outs. Since "being smart" isn't considered very cool at this age, having to miss classes because of the gifted label can become a social burden. This is especially true for girls and minority students. Though this issue is a problem with any type of gifted programming, the nature of pull-out programs seems to emphasize it, regardless of whether the pull-out is for a single period or a day.

Differentiation and Cluster Grouping in the Heterogeneous General Education Classroom

Cluster grouping is the practice of placing small groups of gifted students with a similar strength together within a mixed-ability classroom. It improves the probability that the classroom teacher will take the time to provide alternative instructional activities for them. Teachers use curriculum compacting, accelerated materials, enrichment activities, and independent contracts with students in successful cluster groups. Placing students together in this way more easily allows the gifted resource teacher to schedule time with the teacher and students in order to help plan and support implementation of these activities. It also allows the gifted students to interact with peers of similar ability. They can choose challenging activities without feeling isolated as they tackle them. Cluster grouping can be a significant complement to other services for gifted students (Winebrenner & Devlin, 2001). It can also substitute for an advanced section of a class if there are not enough accelerated students to constitute the whole class.

Differentiation is such an essential practice for gifted students and of such great benefit to all students that it is discussed in detail in Chapter 6.

Grade-Level Acceleration and Coenrollment

One of the most underutilized tools for meeting the needs of gifted students is grade level acceleration. Although there is a popular perception that skipping grades results in children who are socially stunted, half a century of research supports the fact that bright students are often happiest when they are moved forward in schooling and allowed to learn with their intellectual peers (Colangelo, Assouline, & Gross, 2004).

> "America's school system keeps bright students in line by forcing them to learn in a lock-step manner with their classmates. Teachers and principals disregard students' desires to learn more—much more—than they are being taught."
>
> —*A Nation Deceived*, p. 1

Many students could just enter middle school a grade higher, while other gifted students could complete 3 years of middle school in 2 years using careful course combinations so that they meet state and local requirements. Gifted students could also combine their last year of elementary school with the first year of middle school or their last year of middle school with their first year of high school through coenrollment.

Acceleration is appropriate educational planning to match the level and challenge of the curriculum with the readiness and motivation of the students. The Iowa Acceleration Scale (Assouline, Colangelo, Lupkowski-Shoplik, Lipscomb, & Forstadt, 2004) is an information-gathering instrument that provides a sound basis for collaborative decision making about grade-level acceleration. It takes into consideration school, home, psychological, social, and academic factors.

When students are coenrolled in two schools, transportation and distances among school buildings are also factors to consider. It is best to have the student end his or her day at the middle school in order to allow for cocurricular and athletic participation with age (and size!) peers, if appropriate. Therefore, careful advance planning between schools has to take place. For example, if we know that a student needs Honors Algebra II first period at the high school, the high school needs to know this by January of the preceding year in order to create the schedule accordingly.

Good interschool communication can ensure that these individual student articulation issues do not come as a sudden surprise to anyone.

The greatest obstacle to overcome, however, is misunderstanding and myths about the alleged social and emotional cost of grade skipping. The report *A Nation Deceived: How Schools Hold Back America's Brightest Students* (Colangelo et al., 2004) clearly supports grade skipping and describes in detail research demonstrating its success and why it deserves more use. Grade levels, in which students are conveniently organized by their age, are based on a typical intellectual and developmental growth sequence. Gifted students by definition are advanced beyond what would be typical for their age; thus, standard grade-level placements are often inappropriate and restrictive and fail to meet their learning needs and learning pace.

Both grade-based and subject-based acceleration can be powerful tools in meeting the needs of gifted students. They are cost-effective and, when decision making is thorough and includes appropriate follow-up of individual students, serve to advance and enhance students' learning significantly. Individual Written Education Plans (WEPs in some states, IEPs in others) can provide a framework for acceleration and follow-up. Colangelo et al. (2004) cited research suggesting that the few problems that have occurred with acceleration are most often related to incomplete or poor planning.

Competitions, Clubs, Summer Programs, and Distance Learning

In many areas, the only service for gifted and talented students is in after-school or lunchtime clubs and competitions. This is *not* gifted programming, nor does it meet the full educational, social, or emotional needs of gifted students. In the same way that schools provide both gym classes *and* competitive sports, schools must provide both cocurricular academic opportunities and advanced curricula during the school day in order to meet the needs of gifted and talented students.

That being said, there are a great many outstanding cocurricular programs that enhance the school experience for gifted students and provide them with opportunities to engage with the community, find mentors, explore new talents and skills, and socialize with like-minded peers who share their interest. Saturday Exploratory Programs and distance learning (including online courses, correspondence courses, and satellite programs) open up new educational opportunities and study channels for gifted students. There are also many summer programs specifically designed for gifted middle school students. Detailed information about many of these is included in Chapter 9.

Making Decisions

It is not easy to sort through the multiple approaches, program models, and structures to determine what would be the best "fit" for a gifted students in a given school and community. I would encourage a collaborative team of teachers and administrators, including those with expertise in gifted education, to examine what services and structures already exist that are effective and appropriate for gifted and talented students. New planning would determine what is necessary to close the gap between the status quo and the ideal.

The chart on the next page, based on de Bono's PMI thinking strategy, can help in the decision-making process. For each model under consideration, assess what the Pluses might be, what the Minuses might be, and what is just plain Interesting about a particular approach. Then, focused information gathering and planning can take place, as well as exploration of the consequences of implementation and how success will be measured.

	Pluses (Advantages)	Minuses (Disadvantages or Roadblocks)	Interesting Aspects (Worth Investigating)
Magnet School			
School Within a School			
Gifted Team			
Gifted Cluster on a Team			
Gifted/Honors Classes			
Pull-Out Gifted Programming			
Gifted Advisory			
Grade Level Acceleration			
Schoolwide Enrichment Model			
Coenrollment			
Cocurricular Activities, Clubs, Competitions			
Summer or Saturday Programs and/or Distance Learning			

Next Steps . . . Taking Action

1. Determine who should be part of your collaborative team to put a plan together. Consider all stakeholders—including parents, teachers (gifted and regular classroom from the middle and high school), counselors, administrators, and, at a later stage, students.

2. Assess what's already in place and working (foreign language classes, advanced math classes, unified arts classes, high school coenrollment, etc.).

3. Consider school size and community make-up.

4. Collect data on the numbers of identified gifted students in all areas and their needs. Review identification and placement criteria for equity.

5. Assess what personnel are available who have appropriate skills and knowledge of gifted students. Some schools have had great success organizing their program around the strengths of the "right" teacher. Others hire a teacher to supplement existing teachers' strengths. Be sure, however, that there is a gifted advocate/teacher in the building.

6. Examine your team structures and schedules for possible modifications.

7. Assess available financial support—state, local, and national—for program development.

8. Develop a plan for creating a continuum of services.

9. Prepare everyone for changes, including providing appropriate staff development and parent education for everyone who will be affected.

10. Take the leap! Make the changes! It won't be perfect from the start, but you can always revise. The hardest part is making the initial change.

References

Assouline, S., Colangelo, N., Lupkowski-Shoplik, A., Lipscomb, J., & Forstadt, L. (2004). *Iowa Acceleration Scale: A guide to whole-grade acceleration K–8* (2nd ed.). Tucson, AZ: Great Potential Press.

Colangelo, N., Assouline, S. G., & Gross, M. U. M. (2004). *A nation deceived: How schools hold back America's brightest students* (Vol. 1). Iowa City, IA: The Connie Belin & Jacqueline N. Blank International Center for Gifted Education and Talent Development.

Coleman, M. R., Gallagher, J. J., & Howard, J. (1993) *Middle school site visit report: Five schools in profile.* Chapel Hill, NC: Gifted Education Policy Studies Program.

Fiedler, E. D., Lange, R. E., & Winebrenner, S. (1993). *In search of reality: Unraveling the myths about tracking, ability grouping, and the gifted.* Retrieved May 5, 2005, from http://www.tagparents.org/reality.htm

George, P. S. (1997). A second look at grouping, the gifted, and middle school education. In T. O. Erb (Ed.), *Dilemmas in talent development in the middle grades: Two views* (pp. 113–145). Columbus, OH: National Middle School Association.

Kulik, J. A., & Kulik, C. L. (1992). Meta-analytic findings on grouping programs. *Gifted Child Quarterly, 36,* 73–77.

Messick, R. G., & Reynolds, K. E. (1992). *Middle level curriculum in action.* New York: Longman Press.

National Middle School Association. (2003). *This we believe: Successful schools for young adolescents*. Columbus, OH: Author.

Rakow, S. (1994). *Excellence, equity, and empathy: The dilemma of educating the gifted adolescent in the middle school*. Unpublished doctoral dissertation, Kent State University, Kent, OH.

Renzulli, J. S. (1977). *The enrichment triad model: A guide for developing defensible programs for the gifted and talented*. Mansfield Center, CT: Creative Learning Press.

Renzulli, J. S., & Reis, S. M. (n.d.). *What is schoolwide enrichment? And how do gifted programs relate to total school improvement?* Retrieved May 5, 2005, from http://www.sp.uconn.edu/~nrcgt/sem/whatisem.html

Renzulli, J. S., & Reis, S. M. (n.d.). *The Schoolwide Enrichment Model: Executive summary*. Retrieved May 5, 2005, from http://www.sp.uconn.edu/~nrcgt/sem/semexec.html

Rogers, K. (1991, November). The relationship of grouping practices to the education of the gifted and talented learner: Research-based decision making. *NRCG/T Newsletter*. Retrieved May 5, 2005, from http://www.gifted.uconn.edu/nrcgt/newsletter/november91/nov9105.html

Rogers, K. B. (1998). Using current research to make "good" decisions about grouping. *NASSP Bulletin, 82*(595), 38–46.

Slavin, R. E. (1986). *Ability grouping and student achievement in elementary schools: A best evidence synthesis*. Baltimore, MD: Center for Research on Elementary and Middle Schools, Johns Hopkins University.

VanTassel-Baska, J. (n.d.). *Basic educational options for gifted students in schools*. Retrieved May 5, 2005, from http://cfge.wm.edu/documents/Basic_Educational_Options.htm

Winebrenner, S., & Devlin, B. (2001). *Cluster grouping of gifted students: How to provide full-time services on a part-time budget: Update 2001* (ERIC EC Digest #E607). Arlington, VA: The ERIC Clearinghouse on Disabilities and Gifted Education. Retrieved May 5, 2005, from http://www.hoagiesgifted.com/eric/e607.html

Additional Resources

Renzulli, J. S. (1998). A rising tide lifts all ships: Developing the gifts and talents of all students. *Phi Delta Kappan, 80,* 105–111.

Renzulli, J., & Reis, S. M. (1997). Giftedness in middle school students: A talent development perspective. In T. O. Erb (Ed.), *Dilemmas in talent development in the middle grades: Two views* (pp. 43–112). Columbus, OH: National Middle School Association.

The Role of the Gifted Teacher and Intervention Specialist

Essential Questions

1. What qualities contribute to the effectiveness of an intervention specialist/gifted teacher at the middle-grades level?

2. What should the role of intervention specialist/gifted teacher be at the middle-grades level?

"**T**he teacher makes the program."
In my more than 20 years of classroom and professional experiences as a teacher, gifted coordinator, researcher, and consultant, I have heard this over and over again from principals, central office administrators, and parents. A teacher of gifted students must play many roles, especially in a middle school, where all teachers are expected to be part of the learning community—participating on teams, in advisory groups, and in school governance. As a result, it takes a very special individual to be successful as a middle school gifted teacher.

Teacher Qualities

The intense and dynamic balancing act of providing instruction, guidance, and advocacy requires a teacher of gifted students to have unique skills, talents, and personality traits. While many of these qualities are those that should be demonstrated by any good teacher for all students at all levels, some are critical for both effectiveness and survival as a gifted teacher/interventional specialist. Not every teacher is equally effective with all groups of students. In many ways, teachers who do best with gifted students often exhibit many of the students' defining characteristics and cognitive styles themselves and so understand and appreciate them and their families from the inside out (Mills, 2003).

Often based on the mistaken assumption that all gifted students are well-behaved and self-motivated, the common perception is that teaching the gifted is "easier." In reality, it is a complex and constantly demanding endeavor, both in the classroom and in the politically charged arena in which gifted education must often fight for survival. Understanding the qualities necessary for success with gifted students may help school administrators meet the planning and staffing challenge of appropriately matching teachers to gifted programs and students. Consideration of these qualities may also help teachers decide whether they are well-suited for this subspecialty and what professional activities might help them develop necessary attitudes and skills.

Middle school teaching, too, is a specialization that requires certain personalities and skills for success. But, the middle school gifted teacher/intervention specialist must straddle both worlds, gifted education *and* middle school education, on the "front lines" right there in the school. On a daily basis, he or she deals with students, teachers, administrators, counselors, and parents concerned with the academic, intellectual, social, and emotional growth of early adolescents, both gifted and typical. It is a demanding job, one that clearly requires special educators. Often, those who are assigned to teach gifted students in a middle school are those with advanced subject knowledge (e.g., a secondary math or English teacher). This background is necessary, but not sufficient for a gifted teacher to be successful at the middle school level.

Recommendations in *Turning Points 2000* (Jackson & Davis, 2000) and by the National Middle School Association (NMSA; 2003) and the National Association for Gifted Children (NAGC) regarding the qualities of effective teachers are united by each one's acceptance that their specific challenge (teaching gifted students and teaching middle school students) requires individuals with special preparation who also possess particular personal and professional traits. Researchers and experts in both fields have elaborated on these characteristics.

Table 4.1 summarizes and compares the qualities of successful middle school teachers and those of successful teachers of the gifted. It reflects recommendations by NAGC and NMSA, as well as experts in both fields, including Delisle and Lewis (2003), Jackson and Davis (2000), McEwin and Dickinson (2001), Mills (2003), Rogers (2002), Winebrenner (2001), and Wright (1983), as well as gifted students themselves (Heath, 1997).

Perhaps the reason that discussions between these two fields is frequently so heated is their common assertion that passionate commitment to *their* cause (excellent and responsive education for middle school students or gifted students) is *the* most important quality in teachers. The following comment from the NMSA's *This We Believe . . . and Now We Must Act* (Erb, 2003) supporting the need for specially prepared middle-level teachers could have been written by NAGC supporting the need for specially prepared gifted teachers:

> [M]any middle level teachers, and other educators, frequently work intensely in well-intentioned ways that damage rather than enhance the quality of learning opportunities provided for young adolescents. This lack of match between intentions and appropriate behaviors

Table 4.1. Qualities of Successful Middle School Teachers and

	Characteristics of Successful Middle School Teachers
Professional Attributes	• Special preparation to work with this age group • In-depth understanding and knowledge of young adolescents' developmental characteristics and needs and the knowledge and skills to support a safe and healthy school environment for them • A strong conceptual grasp of and advanced coursework in two academic disciplines that can support interdisciplinary curricula and instruction; mastery of the skills to connect these to how early adolescents learn best • Familiar with a wide variety of appropriate teaching strategies, including cooperative learning, problem-based learning, differentiated instruction, and other active and engaging approaches • Understanding of how effective interdisciplinary teams and advisory programs work • Skills in constructing and using a variety of assessment techniques, ranging from traditional testing, to authentic assessments, portfolios, exhibitions, and open-ended problems, and the ability to use ongoing assessment to guide instructional decisions • Understanding of the value of continued professional development and its connection to instructional improvement and student success; a lifelong learner • Capacity to communicate and collaborate with families and community members in support of students and the school • Capability of being effective collaborators who know how to form learning partnerships with their students, other professionals, and parents
Personal Attributes	• "The most important quality middle school teachers bring to their classroom is their commitment to the young adolescents they teach." (NMSA, 2001, p. 11) • A genuine interest in and liking of middle school students; value working with this age and are willing and able to act as advocates, advisors, and mentors • Act as role models, holding high expectations for themselves and their students; dually committed to significant academic learning and developmentally appropriate contexts; demonstrate empathy while engaging students in significant academic learning • Sensitive to individual differences; are supportive and responsive to diversity • Self-understanding, including how they as individuals can best contribute to effective teaming • Flexible • Self-confident • Sense of humor • Value interdisciplinary studies and integrative learning
Political Attributes	• Willingness and preparedness to participate actively in the school's governance system • Willingness and preparedness to advocate for developmentally responsive reforms that benefit middle school students and enhance their achievement and well-being

Successful Teachers of the Gifted

Characteristics of Successful Teachers of the Gifted

- Special preparation in gifted and talented education
- In-depth understanding and knowledge of the special talents, needs, and problems of gifted students and ability to promote a positive self-image among students; are accepting of gifted children and their "quirks"
- Expertise and depth of knowledge in, as well as a passion for, a specific academic area and understanding of the relatedness of knowledge
- Highly developed teaching skills, including knowledge and application of diverse methods that emphasize being a facilitator of learning, rather than a disseminator of knowledge; use of penetrating questions that give students time to think and to express themselves; use of a fast learning pace; enthusiasm for teaching; provide useful and accurate feedback
- Expertise in differentiation of curricula and instruction for gifted, talented, and advanced learners
- Involved in ongoing self-directed professional development, as well as the capability to conduct staff-development sessions within the school and district
- Capacity to communicate and collaborate with families of gifted students and the ability to encourage them to find and take advantage of experiences available for their children through college and community resources

- "The most vital qualification . . . is a personal sense of conviction about the field itself." (Delisle & Lewis, 2003, p. 1)
- A genuine interest in and liking of gifted learners; capacity to advocate for them tirelessly and creatively
- Act as role models for young teens, valuing high standards and achievements, as well as social and emotional well-being that comes from accepting challenges and succeeding; self-directed in their own learning with a love for new, advanced knowledge and learning; recognize the importance of intellectual development—not just interested in "feeling good about yourself" or "classroom community"; capable of sensitively and knowingly responding at gifted children's intellectual level
- Recognize, respect, and believe in individual differences and individualization; support each child's uniqueness; welcome new ways of expression and different opinions
- Self-understanding and emotional maturity
- Flexible, creative, and open-minded; able to suggest new and alternative ways of viewing a problem; high degree of intellectual honesty—able to admit when they don't know something or are wrong and, similarly, understand that even gifted children make mistakes and don't know everything
- Level-headed and emotionally stable—can handle the sensitivity and intensity of gifted youngsters; not easily threatened by a child's disagreement or challenge
- Patient
- Sense of humor
- High degree of intelligence—don't have to be identified gifted, but it is important that they are able to think quickly and use language well
- Possess a wide variety of interests

- Skills in persuasiveness, troubleshooting, problem solving, and finding common ground among disparate voices; possession of a *very* thick skin
- Able and willing to advocate for what gifted students need, including how to apply for funding

rarely results from malice or a lack of caring, but rather is virtually always the result of a lack of knowledge. (p. 15)

Clearly, many of the same qualities that make a good middle school classroom teacher also make a good middle school gifted specialist. There is a great deal of overlap in both the personal and professional domains with regard to the particular populations of 11–14-year-olds and gifted students. There are some differences in the necessary political and advocacy skills, though the often hostile climate that greets reforms in both domains is more similar than different. Intellectual and verbal skills, intensity and understanding of such skills, as well as the ability to respond confidently to the challenges and questioning of gifted students without defensiveness are significant traits for teachers of the gifted. Successful middle school teachers need greater skills in interdisciplinary curricular planning and instruction, teaming, and advisory programs. Middle school teachers' flexibility and their skills in multiple assessment approaches are valuable assets in their work with gifted students.

The success of gifted programming in any middle school revolves around the individual gifted resource specialist. Thoughtful hiring and placement of teachers can help ensure this success.

Teacher Roles

For many people, it is clear what the role of the gifted teacher/intervention specialist is in an elementary school: He or she is involved in testing and identification, as well as direct service to students both in and outside of the regular classroom. Often, the elementary resource specialist also collaborates with classroom teachers to help with differentiation and compacting and, if the Schoolwide Enrichment Model is being used, may direct Type I, II, and III activities.

But in middle schools, the nature of the school's organization and the needs of students, teachers, and administrators are different and so is the role of the gifted teacher. Ideally, each middle school should have its own gifted intervention specialist/gifted teacher. This person may have additional responsibilities (e.g., teaching other classes in his or her area of certification/licensure), but his or her primary role should be to serve as advocate for gifted students while working with their teachers, parents, counselors, and principal. Unfortunately, in too many school districts, gifted personnel travel from building to building and are spread so thin as to be unable to fulfill the multiple aspects of their roles. This becomes a particular liability in middle schools when they are unavailable to participate in essential teaming and faculty collaboration.

Direct Instruction and Support for Gifted Students

The primary responsibility of the middle school gifted teacher should be daily, consistent, coordinated instruction and support of gifted students. This might be through content-based or interdisciplinary classes, pull-out programs, competitions and clubs, or a gifted advisory group. The gifted teacher will seek out and implement appropriate curricula and materials for use in these gifted programs.

Direct student contact should be structured in such a way that teacher and student have the opportunity to get to know each other and build a relationship that will help the teacher provide appropriate guidance and advocacy. In *Turning Points 2000*, Jackson and Davis (2000) recommended, "For young adolescents, relationship with adults form the critical pathways for their learning; education 'happens' through relationships" (p. 121). *This We Believe* (NMSA, 2003) also notes "an adult advocate for every student" (p. 16) as a key component of a successful school for young adolescents. For gifted students, VanTassel-Baska and Baska (1993) stated,

> Teachers with special training in gifted education are needed as much for the affective development of these students as for their cognitive development . . . the teacher of the gifted is uniquely qualified to meet some psychosocial counseling needs of these students. (pp. 181–182)

There are very few counselors specifically trained to deal with the unique needs of gifted students. When they are available, they are shared among several buildings in a district, and most often, they are located at high schools where they provide college, course-scheduling, vocational, testing, and internship advising.

Realistically, the counseling needs of gifted middle school students are met by their gifted teachers. The teachers draw from a variety of strategies to help students understand their uniqueness, survive in intellectually hostile environments, develop appropriate study skills and work habits, get organized in ways consistent with their learning styles, learn social-coping strategies, and plan for their future. Teacher/counselors help gifted students embrace and cope with their differences at a time when pressure for conformity seems to be at its most intense.

> Many gifted students of junior high age, for example, have little idea of appropriate coursework to take as they enter secondary school, particularly as the decision relates to later college and career choices. Teachers can help them plan ahead in their educational experiences in order to maximize potential long-range benefits. The teacher of the gifted can recommend certain types of courses for which the student may be especially well suited, and can point out the importance of such courses, perhaps even based on personal experience. Only if teachers involve themselves in this way can gifted students get the "long view" from someone who knows and understands their needs. (VanTassel-Baska & Baska, 1993, p. 184)

This can also include advising about appropriate online and distance-learning courses and summer programs, as well as scholarship opportunities available to those with limited finances. Though all middle school students need some of this guidance, most are not ready to look this far ahead. Because gifted students may need to accelerate their school placements and learning experiences, it is important for them that this advising take place during middle school, rather than later in their school years.

If a school district has Written Education Plans (WEPs), Guided Learning Plans, or Individual Education Plans (IEPs) for gifted students, the gifted intervention specialist will be responsible for some of these components and may have responsibility for coordinating overall services. This would be one of many collaborations between the gifted teacher and other faculty members.

Faculty Collaboration and Partnerships

The gifted teacher must be a collaborative partner with other faculty and staff in the middle school. Classroom teachers may need help developing and accessing appropriately advanced materials to use with curriculum compacting and differentiation in their classrooms. They may need greater understanding of strategies that work better for gifted students in both academics and their social, emotional, and organizational skill development. During team meetings, the gifted teacher can share his or her understanding of individual gifted students that might help general education teachers be more effective. Contests and summer programs in specific subject areas often come across the desk of the gifted teacher, and these should be shared with subject-specific classroom teachers, who can share them with both identified gifted students and other students in their classes who may be interested or capable.

To the extent possible, having a gifted intervention specialist in a middle school should be seen as offering multiple benefits to the school overall, including a ripple effect that positively impacts the faculty and students throughout the school. Academic competition teams like Knowledge Master Open (KMO) and geography or spelling bees, often sponsored by the gifted teacher or program, should engage interested students from throughout the school population, regardless of formal identification.

Another example occurred when I was the gifted teacher in a middle school. There were students identified as gifted in English/language arts, as well as others who were interested in reading, whose needs were not being adequately met in their English classes. Working with the English department and librarian, I initiated a schoolwide monthly book club. We selected challenging titles, prepared high-level discussion questions, and planned the series for the year. I facilitated the first session so that I could model seminar-type questioning and discussion approaches. Following this, teachers rotated. While many identified gifted students participated, many other middle school students who just loved to read participated and benefited, as well.

Whole-school activities and field trips are other examples of collaboration that benefits the entire school community. When a field trip is planned (like to a theater production or environmental camp or a museum), the gifted teachers can help ensure that higher level thinking and creative thinking are included in preparatory and on-site activities. He or she may also help plan follow-up activities (e.g., speakers, independent projects) for those students whose interest may be whetted by the activity.

Often, gifted teachers and coordinators underestimate the value and power of the teams and teaming within a middle school. Particularly in middle schools where teaching teams are the norm, collaboration with other teachers is a must for the gifted intervention specialist/teacher. Merenbloom (1991) commented that

> Teaming can play a vital role in facilitating the success of handicapped students at this fragile stage of their development . . . the real issue is how to make handicapped

students, teachers of special education classes, and parents of special education students feel worthwhile and included in the mainstream of the middle school experience. (p. 58)

If we substitute *gifted* for *handicapped*, the imperative for including teachers of the gifted in the team process is clear.

Often, no list of identified gifted students is distributed to middle school teachers. IEPs and 504 plans for handicapped students are required by law to be implemented immediately, so all teachers are given lists of students whose learning needs mandate these accommodations. However, it is too often assumed that gifted students will make themselves known to the teacher, thus no notification is provided. Once teachers are informed of those students identified as gifted and their areas of ability or talent (e.g., superior cognitive, math, art), it is more likely that they will encourage and support the advanced performance of which these students are capable. This is especially valuable for African American students (particularly males), underachievers, and twice-exceptional students. So, a significant part of the gifted teacher's responsibility in getting gifted students' needs met is ensuring that all teachers know who the gifted students are. Additionally, he or she should communicate the identification process so teachers can recommend new students or those who may have just begun to show a particular talent. This keeps the door to gifted programming open throughout the middle school years.

The role of the gifted teacher on teams also involves that of "advocate." What is normal for gifted students may not be understood by their teachers, such as doing two things at once (e.g., drawing and listening, reading a book and taking notes). General education teachers may mistakenly characterize gifted students' personal and interpersonal issues such as perfectionism, challenging authority, or lack of organizational skills as a learning disability, a psychological problem, arrogance, or a behavior disorder.

Team meetings usually have several key components:

1. focus on individual students;
2. meeting with parents;
3. planning interdisciplinary instruction and activities;
4. building relationships; and
5. recommendations for schoolwide change/improvement.

Too many time in my visits to middle schools, I have heard gifted teachers comment, "No, I don't attend team meetings—they never talk about *my* kids." There are several problems with this statement. First, despite the fact that the gifted teacher's role is to advocate for gifted students, it is important—especially in middle school—that they not draw lines between "our" and "their" students. If gifted teachers expect classroom teachers to take ownership of some responsibility for teaching gifted students, they have to bring their expertise and understanding to discussions of the rest of the student population, as well. Second, if gifted teachers want to bring up discussions and questions about gifted students and their needs, the team meeting is the place to do it. This is particularly true for twice-exceptional students.

Sometimes during a discussion of a "typical" student, it becomes obvious to the gifted teacher that the troubling behaviors may actually suggest that this is an underachieving gifted student. Strategies that gifted specialists know about or materials that are common in gifted education (like contracts or curriculum compacting) may be helpful to the team. When gifted teachers are aware of what is occurring on a team, they can coordinate their instruction and activities to their students' advantage, to the advantage of other students who may potentially be impacted, and to the school's organization as a whole. And, once the gifted teacher is truly a part of the team, other teachers will be more open and responsive to requests he or she has of them—for curricular adaptations, for not requiring students to make up work when they are pulled out of class, and so forth.

Sometimes, middle schools have events like faculty-student basketball games. To whatever extent is possible and realistic in their lives, gifted teachers should attend (or even participate in) these events. The "elitist" label sticks when gifted teachers are too busy or seem to be "above" contributing to the life of the school as a whole. It is important to know and understand the school and how it works, to have relationships with the faculty and students, and to collaborate on building a developmentally responsive middle school that works for gifted students.

Participating in team meetings, working on all-school activities, helping individual teachers meet the needs of specific students, and attending occasional social events helps break down barriers and creates an environment that says, "I am a committed faculty member of this middle school along with everyone else."

In-Service and Staff Development

Particularly in an era when school funds are limited, gifted intervention specialists and district coordinators may be asked to provide in-service programs and staff development in a variety of forms for their own schools.

For most teachers, this is not something they were trained to do. Despite having participated in staff-development programs, many teachers are unfamiliar with how presentations should be structured for the greatest impact on adult learners. Sometimes, too, there is resentment from colleagues, particularly if there isn't adequate administrative support and follow-up.

Nevertheless, the responsibility for helping general education teachers and support personnel (e.g., coaches, librarians) understand and meet the needs of gifted students frequently falls to the middle school's gifted teacher as an expected part of his or her job. Team meetings, one-to-one coaching or mentoring, or specific topics for schoolwide faculty meetings can all be used to provide this information. Currently, differentiation of instruction seems to be a topic of particular interest to teachers and administrators at the middle school level since it presumes a heterogeneous class.

Additional support for individual teachers can sometimes be offered by providing unit enrichment activities, suggesting alternative advanced materials, or coteaching. General education teachers are often not familiar with the publishers of materials especially designed or adaptable for gifted students. Working with classroom teachers to implement simulations or small-group differentiated activities can help them build the confidence they need to continue to implement these strategies on their own. It also keeps the gifted teacher grounded in the reality of the typical classroom environment and builds his or her real-world credibility with other faculty, who often assume that his or her only teaching occurs in the "rarified" atmosphere of a gifted class.

A variety of materials are available to teachers who find themselves thrust into the role of staff developer. *Staff Development: The Key to Effective Gifted Education Programs* (Dettmer & Landrum, 1998) provides assistance in both planning and facilitating gifted staff development, the effectiveness of which is enhanced when it occurs in the actual school where gifted education programs are to be implemented because it can then be supported by long-term relationships and daily connections. Dettmer and Landrum provide guidance for development and implementation of needs assessments, as well as measures of accountability and evaluation.

Leadership for Differentiating Schools and Classrooms (Tomlinson & Allan, 2000) also has helpful suggestions that can apply across a broader spectrum of strategies for which teachers may be asked to provide in-service assistance. Staff development on differentiation should:

- build a common vocabulary related to differentiation;
- attend to teachers' levels of readiness (information, comprehension, skills, commitment), interest, and preferred learning modes;

- offer options directly focused on particular needs of particular grade levels and subject areas;
- include school administrators and other district leaders in the planning;
- consistently emphasize high-quality curricula and instruction as the starting point for meaningful differentiation;
- be planned to ensure transfer of knowledge, understanding, and skill into the classroom;
- be aligned with other school, district, and state goals and outcomes;
- include ways to recognize teachers' efforts; and
- be differentiated based on teacher proficiency and comfort with the topic (pp. 79–82).

The Association for Supervision and Curriculum Development (ASCD) has a complete kit with videos and facilitator guide on differentiating instruction that lends itself to engaged participation by individuals, small study groups, and whole faculty sessions (see http://shop.ascd.org/ProductDisplay.cfm?Product ID=104467). A wider range of topics is covered in the "Big Red Notebook" entitled *Applying Gifted Education Pedagogy in the General Education Classroom: Professional Development Module* (Burns et al., 2002). This kit includes overheads, activity pages, and facilitator discussion guide.

The most specific assistance, however, may be found in *Consultation in Gifted Education: Teachers Working Together to Serve Students* (Landrum, 2002). This practical guide is directed at developing collaboration programs with a clear intent:

> specialists and generalists combine efforts and expertise to accomplish more in the education of gifted learners. The participating staff become more knowledgeable and therefore more effective in their subsequent interactions with and instruction of gifted learners in their classrooms. (p. 3)

Landrum emphasizes what teachers in the field have already accepted in other areas of special education: that both general educators and gifted specialists share responsibility for designing educational services for gifted learners through dialogue and collaborative planning. The book also provides case studies of lessons and classrooms at a variety of grade levels.

The issue of time, however, is critical. If middle school gifted intervention specialists are expected to provide schoolwide staff development, one-to-one mentoring, and other classroom-based follow-up, they must have time built into their schedules for planning and coaching. It cannot just be added on to other, more typical teacher responsibilities (e.g., day-to-day planning and instruction of gifted students, attending team meetings, grading, parent contact).

Parent Relationships and Education

Many parents are confused about how to assist and advocate for their gifted child once he or she reaches his or her early teens. So, another responsibility for the middle school gifted intervention specialist is that of parent education. The social, emotional, and academic changes of early adolescence often take parents of gifted teens by surprise. Many parents understood their role more clearly when their child was younger, both at home and at school. The middle school gifted teacher often provides informal parent guidance on the phone, through newsletters and meetings, and at more formal parent conferences. Parents can be directed to local support and advocacy groups or those available through NAGC or SENG (Supporting Emotional Needs of the Gifted).

Like other parents of youngsters with special needs, parents of gifted students must be encouraged to be involved and advocate for their children during middle school. The gifted resource teacher can help parents feel comfortable coming to school and can provide guidance in negotiating an individual school or district's internal power structure.

Additionally, the gifted teacher is often the conduit for information about summer programs, online courses, arts events and classes, high school and college course selections, and competition, mentorship, and publication opportunities. The need for these and availability vary by school, district, location, and individual student.

Gifted Advocacy

Another important lesson learned from other special education professionals is the vital role of advocacy. Gifted students need professionals to speak out on their behalf at district-level curriculum and planning meetings, school and team meetings, articulation meetings (middle to high school, elementary to middle school), PTA events, and any other opportunities that present themselves. Sometimes, all it takes is raising questions, such as "What accommodations does this textbook series provide for gifted and advanced students?" or "What impact will that schedule change have on gifted programming?" Other times, advocacy means standing up for a student at a team meeting and defending his or her behavior as typical of middle school gifted children whose needs are not being met. Sometimes, it involves going to see the principal or counselor along with parents who have legitimate concerns about their child's academic progress. Occasionally, it is helping gather necessary information to support a decision on grade-level or subject acceleration, including the research support when these decisions fly in the face of popular mythology (e.g., "early ripe, early rot," "disastrous social consequences").

The most common advocacy is meeting with a teacher on a student's behalf or with both teacher and student in order to negotiate reasonable classroom accommodations. Many individuals need help understanding dual exceptionality ("Yes, an LD student can also be gifted"), perfectionism, underachievement, or asynchronous development and how schools can address gifted students' needs in the social/emotional domains. This can combat the "he or she doesn't deserve to go to the gifted program" mentality that often deprives students of needed services. Because most middle school teachers and administrators see themselves as student advocates, this role may not be new for those with years of experience. But, it is often uncomfortable to go against the prevailing opinions, attitudes, and practices of a given middle school to advocate for gifted students and the issues that affect them. Being sure to have the right kind of teacher in this position is the first step to ensuring that students will have a passionate and committed spokesperson on their side.

Next Steps . . . Taking Action

1. Select a teacher with the appropriate skills, knowledge, understanding, experience, and personality for the challenges of the job. The "right person" is at least half of a good program.

2. Provide a schedule that allows the middle school gifted intervention specialist the time necessary to fulfill the multiple roles that are expected, including attendance at team meetings.

References

Burns, D. E., Gubbins, E. J., Reis, S. M., Westberg, K. L., Dinnocenti, S. T., & Tieso, C. L. (2002). *Applying gifted education pedagogy in the general education classroom: Professional development module.* Storrs: National Research Center on the Gifted and Talented, University of Connecticut.

Delisle, J., & Lewis, B. A. (2003). *The survival guide for teachers of gifted kids: How to plan, manage, and evaluate programs for gifted youth K–12.* Minneapolis, MN: Free Spirit Press.

Dettmer, P., & Landrum, M. (1998). *Staff development: The key to effective gifted education programs.* Waco, TX: Prufrock Press.

Erb, T. O. (Ed.). *This we believe . . . and now we must act.* Westerville, OH: National Middle School Association.

Heath, W. J. (1997). *What are the most effective characteristics of teachers of the gifted?* (ERIC Document Reproduction Service No. ED 411665)

Jackson, A. W., & Davis, G. A. (2000). *Turning points 2000: Educating adolescents in the 21st century.* New York: Teachers College Press.

Landrum, M. S. (2002). *Consultation in gifted education: Teachers working together to serve students.* Mansfield Center, CT: Creative Learning Press.

McEwin, C. K., & Dickinson, C. K. (2001). Educators committed to young adolescents. In T. O. Erb (Ed.), *This we believe . . . and now we must act* (pp. 11–19). Westerville, OH: National Middle School Association.

Merenbloom, E. Y. (1991). *The team process: A handbook for teachers* (3rd ed.). Columbus, OH: National Middle School Association.

Mills, C. J. (2003). Characteristics of effective teachers of gifted students: Teacher background and personality styles of students. *Gifted Child Quarterly, 47,* 272–281.

National Middle School Association. (2003). *This we believe: Successful schools for young adolescents.* Westerville, OH: Author.

Rogers, K. (2002). *Re-forming gifted education: How parents and teachers can match the program to the child.* Scottsdale, AZ: Great Potential Press.

Thompson, S. C. (Ed.). (2004). *Reforming middle level education: Considerations for policymakers.* Greenwich, CT: Information Age.

Tomlinson, C. A., and Allan, S. D. (2000). *Leadership for differentiating schools and classrooms.* Alexandria, VA: Association for Supervision and Curriculum Development.

Van Tassel-Baska, J., & Baska, L. (1993). The role of educational personnel in counseling the gifted. In L. K. Silverman (Ed.), *Counseling the gifted and talented* (pp. 181–200). Denver, CO: Love.

Winebrenner, S. (2001). *Teaching gifted kids in the regular classroom: Strategies and techniques every teacher can use to meet the academic needs of the gifted and talented* (Rev. ed.). Minneapolis, MN: Free Spirit Press.

Wright, J. D. (1983). *Teaching the gifted and talented in the middle school.* Washington, DC: National Education Association.

Curricular and Instructional Strategies

Essential Questions

1. What elements should distinguish effective curricula for gifted students in middle school?

2. What instructional strategies are most effective for gifted students in middle school?

For many years, gifted education and middle school education have both borne the accusation of spending too much time on program structure and not enough on what happens for students, what one National Middle School Association (NMSA) book called "the 'absent presence' of the curriculum question" (Beane, 1990, p. 1).

For middle schools, this meant schools focused on establishing interdisciplinary teams and teaming, advisory programs, and other school organization issues. James Beane (2004), one of the foremost scholars and thinkers on the issue of middle school curricula, commented, "the lack of an appropriate curriculum continues to frustrate the lives of young adolescents and a great many of the adults who live and work with them in school and at home" (p. 50).

In gifted education, this "absent presence" manifests in endless debates on identification and placement criteria, as well as pull-out versus self-contained programs versus differentiation in the general education classroom versus special schools versus whole-school enrichment versus grade acceleration. But, the most significant question for gifted students is "What happens *in* their classes and programs?"

Recent voices in middle level education (e.g., Anfara, 2004; Beane, 2004; George, 1997; Jackson & Davis, 2000; Stevenson, 2001) reflect similar concern about what happens in classes for *all* middle school students, particularly under the influence of the No Child Left Behind Act and accountability testing. "If current trends persist, we will soon be able to describe the middle school curriculum as a collection of test-driven content and skills isolated in separate subject classes and superficially covered by teachers using standardized methods and materials" (Beane, p. 61).

In *This We Believe* (National Middle School Association, 2003) and *This We Believe . . . And Now We Must Act* (Erb, 2001), middle school advocates assert that middle school curricula should be challenging, integrated, exploratory, and designed specifically to ensure the healthy development of young adolescent learners. Additionally, they support

- rigorous academic standards of excellence;
- curricula that are concerned with essential concepts, themes, and problems of the disciplines, as well as their interdisciplinary and integrated connections;
- curricula that incorporate authentic learning and assessment;
- "place-based" curricula (i.e., work that is connected to particular community contexts); and
- curricula that are developmentally responsive and socially conscious.

In *Turning Points 2000*, Jackson and Davis (2000) suggest Wiggins and McTighe's (1998) *Understanding by Design* as one possible model for designing instruction appropriate for middle-grades students because of its emphasis on both subject exploration and student motivation. Lounsbury and Vars (1978) encouraged the use of problem-centered core curriculum programs.

Many of these curricular goals are consistent with the needs of gifted middle school students. Both the National Association for Gifted Children (NAGC) and The Association for Gifted (TAG), a division of the Council for Exceptional Children (CEC), offer general standards for gifted curricula that can be used to guide decisions for particular content areas and grade levels. Each individual subject area association also has curriculum guidelines for various grade levels.

Choice and Challenge: The Keys to Effective Curricula for Gifted Students

During adolescence, the brain will decline in plasticity but increase in power, and a boring environment will have a more powerful thinning effect on the cortex than the thickening effect of the enriched environment. During this period, gifted students are very susceptible to losing mental ground when not challenged. (Clark, 2002, p. 209)

Both choice and challenge are essential to appropriate curricula for gifted students. *Choice* means actively engaging students in collaborative decisions with faculty about what they will study, the pace and methods of study, and how they will share what they've learned. *Challenge* has three major components: acceleration, depth, and complexity.

The curricular models described in this chapter incorporate both choice and challenge in various ways and to varying degrees. Some emphasize one aspect over the other. Some are embedded in a particular program structure, while others can be incorporated into a variety of structures, including differentiated general education classes.

Gifted programming should not exist in a vacuum. Decision makers need to consider how each particular curricular model can fit into specific school and community contexts while incorporating or reflecting mandated national, state, and local standards.

What Not to Do

**Don't make external structural changes
without substantive content change.**

No structural change is enough by itself. Ability grouping without a change in materials, content, or instruction does not address students' needs. Some schools, in an attempt to decrease perceived elitism in advanced or gifted classes, mandate that such classes use the same text and content used in general education classes. Some individual teachers also do this in order to simplify their multiple preparations. But, this defeats the academic purpose of the grouping (though some of the social/emotional needs can still be met this way), which is to provide more advanced content at a faster pace. In order for gifted students to maximize their potential, something different has to happen for them whether they are in the general education classroom, a gifted pull-out program, or an advanced class.

The move toward inclusion classrooms places demands on teachers that may diminish their resources (human and material) to address the needs of gifted students. Classes may be slowed down even further and content made even more "basic" to allow for the involvement, success, and acceptance of inclusion students. Even grade-level acceleration with no change in pace or content may not meet the needs of gifted students. So, in order for schooling to be more appropriate for gifted middle school students, there should be thoughtful comprehensive accommodations in both curricula and instruction.

Don't ignore standards.

The current educational and political climate requires that all teachers and students be accountable for certain levels of proficiency in various content areas. In order to meet these accountability demands and justify alternative activities and content for gifted students, state and local standards should be embedded in instructional planning. This can occur through preassessment (to document student mastery of the standards before alternative instruction begins) or through the design of curricula that incorporate the standards into learning activities and outcomes.

To me, the difference between standards-embedded and standards-based curricula is the starting point: Do you start with instruction focused on a single particular standard (i.e., use of commas, multiplication of fractions), or do you embed it in a larger activity (e.g., creating a newspaper for a particular novel's historical period or calculating recipes for a Renaissance Faire feast)? The former would be standards-based, and the latter would be standards-embedded.

Teachers should be able to provide evidence of individual students' levels of mastery on standards relevant to their grade and subject area. In addition, above-grade-level standards can be used to increase challenge and provide accelerated learning opportunities, and mastery of them should also be documented. The political realities of standardized testing and accountability in America in the early 21st century require this.

**Don't continue elementary programs
unchanged for middle school students.**

The self-contained classrooms and overall structure of elementary schools often allow for connected exploration of content and more individualized learning. There may be physical space for setting up long-term learning centers and independent study carrels. But, middle school schedules, shared classrooms, and organizational structures frequently limit some instructional options for gifted students, although they provide an optimum environment for others.

In addition, adolescents respond differently than younger children to various learning experiences. For example, some districts have elementary gifted students leave their building for a day or a half day for specialized programming. But, adolescents may not want to miss that amount of time with their friends, face the inevitable make-up work, deal with the social consequences of the obvious labeling and separation, or possibly miss an athletic event.

Before extending even a successful elementary gifted program into a middle school, questions about its appropriateness to adolescents and the middle school structure in each unique community context must be addressed.

Don't misuse hands-on and cooperative learning with gifted students.

Many teachers misunderstand and misapply hands-on learning experiences. For typical students, these activities provide the bridge from Piaget's concrete learning stage to formal operations or abstract concepts and can provide positive social experiences. However, for many gifted students who have already mastered a particular concept, the hands-on practice may not be a good use of their time, particularly in cooperative learning groups where they are consistently the smartest student. This is particularly true in some science and math classrooms where manipulatives are used in groups to teach or review concepts or operations gifted students already know. So, what the gifted student actually learns is "Go through the motions anyway."

Those who refuse to conform to this often stop working, and we see misbehavior and some of the causes of underachievement (which is rampant in this age group, particularly with males): boredom, repetition, and lack of challenge. George (1997) commented, "Cooperative learning, peer tutoring, and other models of instruction, when used ineffectively in middle school, may too often place the gifted student in the role of tutor, giving at least the impression of impeding their academic progress in favor of remediating the slower students" (p. 115). (For more on cooperative learning and gifted students, see Chapter 2.)

Curricular Models

As in all aspects of education, teachers and administrators use professional judgment to guide decision making. All of these strategies, models, and approaches are useful and valuable, and they should not be perceived as mutually exclusive in one school or even in one subject area. The key is to make choices based on appropriateness to the students, to the individual school, and to the broader community context. It is also important to consider the transitional role that middle schools play in school districts so that programming clearly connects a particular district's elementary and high school curricula.

Pre-AP and Pre-IB

The Advanced Placement (AP) and International Baccalaureate (IB) programs are rigorous and accelerated programs designed for high school students. When these are available in a district's high school, advanced classes for gifted middle school students may be part of an articulated preparatory sequence.

The College Board's Advanced Placement program recommends the establishment of vertical teacher teams in grades 6–12 that can plan instruction to help students be successful when they actually reach the AP classes. These teams create a pre-AP curriculum appropriate to an individual school or district that is also inclusive of the prerequisite knowledge and skills for AP courses. Materials and workshops are available for teachers in math, social studies, English/language arts, and the fine arts. The focus for workshop participants is on professional development in teaching strategies and pedagogical issues. Additional information on pre-AP curricula can be found at http://apcentral.collegeboard.com.

While pre-AP is focused on teachers, the International Baccalaureate's Middle Years Programme (MYP) is an actual curriculum for students 11–16 years old. The 5-year MYP curriculum can be used in conjunction with or independent of the high school Diploma Programme and the elementary Primary Years Programme. The focus is on developing students who have deeper global understanding and strong abilities in languages. Responsive to the developmental needs of adolescents, it incorporates interdisciplinary curricula and active learning strategies. The academic framework includes courses in eight areas: two languages (the native language and one other), mathematics, sciences, humanities, arts, technology, and physical education. There is also a community service component and an Approaches to Learning course. All students complete a rigorous and extensive personal project in their last year. The program allows enough flexibility to incorporate state and local standards and assessments. Schools must apply and be approved for participation in all levels of IB. Additional information on pre-IB curricula can be found at http://www.ibo.org.

The Autonomous Learner Model (ALM)

Designed by George Betts specifically for gifted students, the Autonomous Learner Model (ALM; see Figure 5.1), contains five dimensions:

- Orientation (self-understanding related to the fundamental concepts of giftedness, talent, intelligence, creativity, and the development of potential);

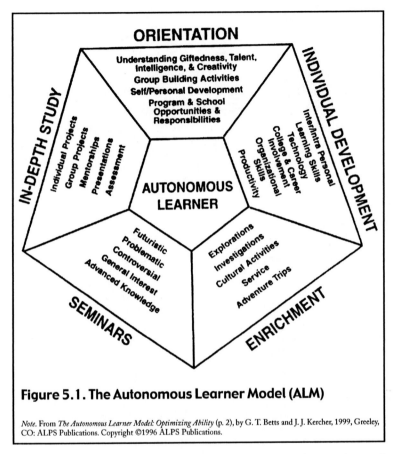

Figure 5.1. The Autonomous Learner Model (ALM)

- Individual Development (development of attitudes and skills for autonomous life-long learning);
- Enrichment (exploration of areas and topics not typically part of the school's curriculum);
- Seminar (group research, presentation, and assessment); and
- In-Depth Study (long-term individual independent investigation).

In all dimensions, the goal is for individuals to move from "student" to "autonomous learner," increasing awareness of one's self and one's abilities and motivation to actively and independently pursue self-directed, personally significant learning. The role of the teacher in this model is that of facilitator and advisor.

While the program can be applied to students in grades K–12, many aspects of it are especially appropriate for middle schools, where the dimensions can intersect seamlessly with existing curricula and programming. The ALM can be part of an advisory program for gifted students, provide the framework for a gifted pull-out program, be incorporated in an Advanced English or reading (or other subject area) class, or be an exploratory class in itself. For more information on the ALM, see Betts and Kercher (1999).

Academies of Inquiry and Talent Development (AITD)

Developed by Joseph Renzulli, Academies of Inquiry and Talent Development (AITD) evolved from the enrichment cluster component of the Schoolwide Enrichment Model (SEM). Though not specifically designed for gifted students, many aspects of the AITD can benefit them. Like the SEM, an AITD is

> not intended to replace or minimize existing services to high achieving students . . . its purpose is to integrate these services into a "rising-tide-lifts-all-ships" approach to school improvement and to expand the role of enrichment specialists by having these persons infuse specific practices for high-end learning into the total school program. (Renzulli & Reis, 1997, p. 89)

In the academies, the emphasis is on real-world problem solving in self-selected learning communities that focus on specific subjects or interest areas (e.g., physical and life sciences, fine and performing arts). The academies are designed to promote academic rigor through instructional differentiation. The model can be part of an exploratory or advisory program, or it can be the organizing structure for an activity period. Teachers and students remain as part of one academy for several years, allowing for the cultivation of sustained personal relationships between teachers and students. Multiage and multigrade interactions, as well as the interdisciplinary nature of the projects tackled in the academies, can benefit gifted students. Inquiry is structured around Type I, II, and III enrichment activities (see Chapter 3 for more description of these and the SEM). For more information on AITD, see Renzulli (2000, 2001).

The Parallel Curriculum Model (PCM)

In answer to how curricula for gifted students should differ, the Parallel Curriculum Model (PCM; see Figure 5.2) was developed by some of the best thinkers and educators in the field of gifted education: Carol Ann Tomlinson, Sandra Kaplan, Joseph Renzulli, Jeanne Purcell, Jann Leppien, and Deborah Burns. It proposes four strands that synthesize key components of a quality curriculum for high-potential and high-ability learners: the Curriculum of Connections, the Curriculum of Identity, the Core Curriculum, and the Curriculum of Practice.

The curriculum is not really parallel in the sense of *parallel* meaning two or more lines or planes that do not intersect. By other definitions of *parallel*, however, the descriptor is perfect: "Having readily recognized similarities, analogous aspects, or comparable parts. . . . Having the same direction or tendency" (*Webster's II New College Dictionary*, 1999). Actually, I see it as a "lasagna" curriculum in which each layer enhances those above and below it and they all mingle to create a rich new whole.

The Core Curriculum is the high-level disciplinary or interdisciplinary content based on the essential questions to be answered in a unit of study. This includes goals and objectives, as well as materials and assessments. The Curriculum of Connections is the content and processes that build bridges between the Core Curriculum and other disciplines, time periods,

The Core or Basic Curriculum	The Curriculum of Connections
The Core Curriculum is the foundational curriculum that establishes a rich framework of knowledge, understanding, and skills most relevant to the discipline. It is inclusive of and extends state and district expectations. It is the starting point or root system for all of the parallels in this model. The Core or Basic Curriculum: • Is built on key facts, concepts, principles, and skills essential to discipline • Is coherent in its organization • Is purposefully focused and organized to achieve essential outcomes • Promotes understanding rather than rote learning • Is taught in a meaningful context • Causes students to grapple with ideas and questions, using both critical and creative thinking • Is mentally and affectively engaging and satisfying to learners • Results in evidence of worthwhile student production	This curriculum is derived from and extends the Core Curriculum. It is designed to help students encounter and interact with the key concepts, principles, and skills in a variety of settings, times, and circumstances. The Curriculum of Connections is designed to help students think about and apply key concepts, principles, and skills: • In a range of instances throughout the discipline • Across disciplines • Across time and time periods • Across locations • Across cultures • Across times, locations, and cultures • Through varied perspectives • As impacted by various conditions (social, economic, technological, political, etc.) • Through the eyes of various people who affected and are affected by the ideas • By examining links between concepts and development of the disciplines

Figure 5.2. The Parallel Curriculum Model (PCM)

cultures and locations, subtopics, and perspectives. The Curriculum of Practice expands the Core Curriculum to help students learn how to behave as scholars and producers in a discipline and to explore the real-world applications of their learning. The Curriculum of Identity invites students to connect the other three strands to themselves as unique individuals with skills, interests, behaviors, and values. Here students investigate their role in the world as related to this particular unit of study and question the possible long-term implications of their involvement with this discipline or topic.

Each strand is developed by asking questions in 10 key foundation areas that are the same for all the parallels: specific content, assessment, introduction, teaching strategies, learning activities, grouping formats, products, resources, extension activities, and ascending levels of intellectual demand. Rather than serving as a program itself, the PCM provides a framework for developing units or for reviewing existing curricula for appropriateness for gifted students.

Figure 5.3 contains graphic representations of this dynamic process. At the core, or heart, of the PCM are the balance of yin and yang, the balance of core content (knowledge, understanding, and skills) with students (needs, abilities, and interests). While separate, consideration of one is embedded in the other (note the black-and-white circles within each contrasting side of the diagram's center.) What unites the two sides are carefully selected essential questions—issues that are of concern and importance to both the discipline(s) and the students. It is a wavy line because, for some topics, there is greater emphasis on the student aspect, while for others, there is greater emphasis on the content aspect. Around this (and you'll have to use your imagination a bit here) revolves the curriculum circle segments of Practice, Identity, and Connections (described above). As each segment is considered, the 10 foundational components are created or reviewed. For example, when considering the Curriculum of Identity, teachers would ask

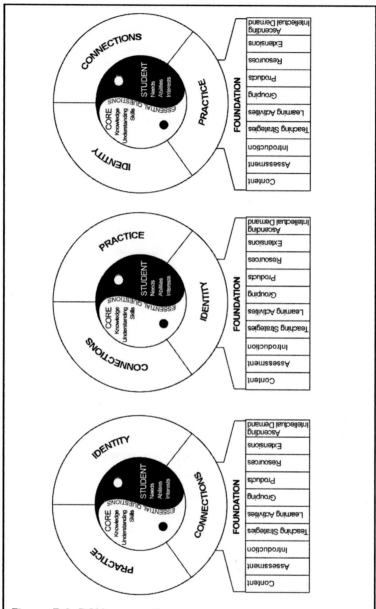

Figure 5.3. PCM connections

Note. Many thanks to my colleague, Robert Davis, at Beachwood Middle School for transferring my sketched design into this computer graphic.

- What content reflects questions of identity?
- What provisions are there in the unit for ascending levels of intellectual demand so that the unit will meet the range of my students?
- How will I introduce this aspect of the unit?
- What teaching strategies, learning activities, and grouping strategies will be most effective with my students?
- What assessment tools are appropriate and when should they be used?
- What products might students create that would best demonstrate their understanding of the Curriculum of Identity?
- What resources do we need for this unit?
- What opportunities for extensions need to be developed for this unit?

Then, the curriculum circle rotates, placing the Curriculum of Connections segment over the Foundation Components and the same questions are asked. When the core content of a unit is planned, teachers also ask the same 10 questions.

When I used this approach with colleagues as a lens for reviewing existing curricula in the gifted program I designed at Beachwood Middle School in Ohio, I discovered that the Curriculum of Practice was weak in most units. In collaboration with the teachers and the PCM text (Tomlinson et al., 2002), we brainstormed how we could improve our units to make them more active and relevant in this area. We accomplished this by adding more out-of-school experiences and bringing more guest speakers into the school.

It is clear how the PCM fits into the middle school models of curricula proposed by Beane (2004) and others. It includes developmentally appropriate investigations into identity, core content and interdisciplinary connections, and real-world applications, and it provides an opportunity for differentiating to meet varying student needs. Whether used alone in a self-contained gifted classroom or as part of a general education classroom, the PCM is a powerful tool for teachers and administrators. It can meet Beane's criteria of being academically challenging and intellectually stimulating, developmentally responsive and respectful, and socially equitable and conscious while providing gifted students with the challenge and choices they need. It also seems well suited to another essential component of good middle school curricula: interdisciplinary connections.

Bloom's Taxonomy: An Oldie, But Goodie . . . and Now Even Better

The easiest and most basic way to begin thinking about curriculum design for gifted and talented students is with Bloom's taxonomy. Each level describes increasingly more complex thinking and learning tasks. This model was designed by Benjamin Bloom and associates in the 1950s, expanded into the affective domain by Bloom, Krathwohl, and Masia in the 1960s, and most recently revised in 2001 by Anderson (a former student of Bloom's) and Krathwohl. It is a staple of teacher-preparation programs and curriculum designers. It tends to fade into memory, however, as busy teachers become involved in day-to-day classroom work and face the looming presence of external standards and assessments.

The most recent revision includes some renaming (as active verbs) and reorganizing in order to better reflect the active nature of thinking processes and the more highly complex nature of creative thinking over critical thinking (see Figure 5.4).

In addition, the revised taxonomy adds a second dimension: knowledge dimensions, the kind of knowledge to be learned. These include factual knowledge, conceptual knowledge, procedural knowledge, and meta-cognitive knowledge, each of which can be applied to the six dimensions of cognitive processing. The revision provides a more useful tool for curriculum planning, teaching, and assessment (see Figure 5.5).

Remember (formerly Knowledge)	Asking students to simply recall and recognize facts, details, parts, theories, and so forth without alteration; retrieve relevant knowledge from long-term memory.
Understand (formerly Comprehension)	Asking students to demonstrate basic understanding of a topic, concept, structure, and so forth without deep implications or complexities. Includes paraphrasing, exemplifying, classifying, summarizing, inferring from examples, comparing, and explaining.
Apply (formerly Application)	Asking students to apply generalizations, abstractions, methods, theories, procedures, and/or rules in specific situations. Includes executing and implementing.
Analyze (formerly Analysis)	Asking students to take apart ideas, structures, texts, and so forth and explain the component parts and their relationship to each other and to the whole. Includes differentiating, organizing, and attributing (i.e., point of view.)
Evaluate (formerly Evaluation)	Asking students to use particular criteria (either developed by or given to the student) to evaluate, judge, critique, or assess an idea, product, approach, and so forth.
Create (formerly Synthesis)	Asking students to use separate knowledge and understandings to create a coherent, organized whole or new relationship that did not previously exist; combining elements into a pattern not clearly there before.

Figure 5.4. Bloom's taxonomy of cognitive processes

Note. Adapted from *A Taxonomy for Learning, Teaching, and Assessing: A Revision of Bloom's Taxonomy of Educational Objectives* (p. 67–68), by L. W. Anderson and D. R. Krathwohl, 2001, New York: Longman. Copyright ©2001 by Longman.

The Knowledge Dimension	The Cognitive Process Dimension					
	Remember	Understand	Apply	Analyze	Evaluate	Create
Factual Knowledge						
Conceptual Knowledge						
Procedural Knowledge						
Meta-cognitive Knowledge						

Figure 5.5. Knowledge dimensions of Bloom's taxonomy

Note. From "Bloom's Revised Taxonomy," by E. Cruz, 2002, *Encyclopedia of Educational Technology.* Retrieved May 12, 2005, from http://coe.sdsu.edu/eet/Articles/index.htm. Copyright ©2002 by San Diego State University.

When Tomlinson and others speak of adding depth and complexity to the curriculum, Bloom's taxonomy is an easy and obvious place to start. All students can and should have opportunities for thinking and learning at the higher levels. However, gifted students, due to their rapid learning pace or prior knowledge, should spend less time at the three basic levels and more time at the three more advanced levels (see Figure 5.6). These levels can

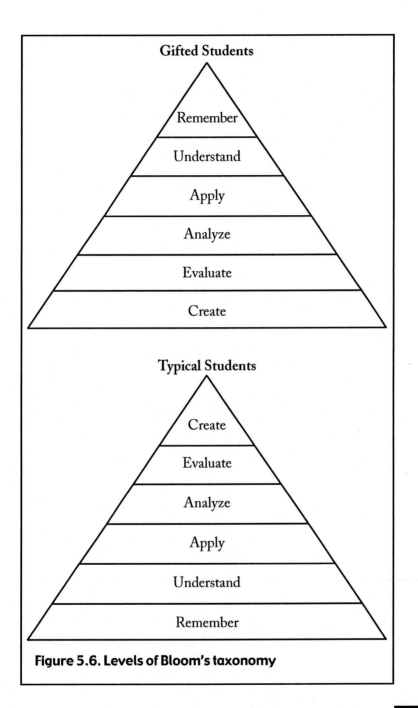

Figure 5.6. Levels of Bloom's taxonomy

provide teachers and curriculum planners with guidance in designing tiered assignments, enrichment activities, accelerated opportunities, mastery learning, curriculum compacting, menu-model components, lesson plans, and differentiated homework assignments.

The Curry/Samara Model (CSM)

The Curry/Samara Model (CSM) is based on three dimensions of the curriculum: content, process, and product. The process strand uses six cognitive levels based on Bloom's (1956) earlier taxonomy. The first three are categorized as "Basic Thinking" and follow Bloom exactly (knowledge, comprehension, and application.) The latter three, collectively called "Abstract Thinking" include Bloom's analysis level, but Curry and Samara substitute the terms "creative thinking" and "critical thinking" for "synthesis" and "evaluation."

Though not specifically designed for gifted students, CSM's differentiated approach to curricula and its emphasis on "big ideas" and interdisciplinary connections make it a good fit for gifted middle school students. The adaptations in instruction and assessment are compatible with either a self-contained advanced class or meeting the needs of gifted students in a heterogeneous grouping. Using a matrix (see Figure 5.7), teachers design a comprehensive unit of study that includes a content outline, state standards, thinking processes, and student assessment using both traditional and authentic methods.

In addition, the CSM incorporates affective goals in the areas of feelings, beliefs, perceptions, and attitudes in order to connect content to students, which makes this model valuable for gifted students during their early adolescence when it is all too easy for them to be caught by the "grade game," (focusing on points earned or minimum requirements for an A grade), rather than being engaged in meaningful and rewarding learning experiences.

Arctic National Wildlife Refuge	Basic Thinking			Analysis	Abstract Thinking	
	Knowledge	Comprehension	Application		Creative Thinking	Critical Thinking
1. Natural Resources of Arctic Slope a. petroleum b. coal c. natural gas d. gold/silver e. fish f. fur	1a. Locate petroleum sites through a map.	2a. Describe how an oil rig works through a demonstration.	3a. Organize the annual production rates of natural resources through a bar graph.	4a. Determine the order of the importance of resources to ANWR through a class discussion.	5a. Elaborate on the use and value of petroleum in ANWR through a commercials.	6a. Judge which resource would be most important to ANWR through a round table discussion.
2. Wildlife of Arctic Slope a. animals b. birds c. sea life	7a. Recognize animals, birds and sea life of ANWR through a content puzzle.	8a. Explain the migration routes of the caribou through a map.	9a. Summarize the life cycles of ANWR wildlife through a public service announcement.	10a. Compare the impact of oil drilling on wildlife through a poster.	11a. Speculate how an animal's life cycle might change after oil drilling through a cartoon.	12a. Justify a pro/con viewpoint about ANWR drilling through a persuasive letter.
3. Indigenous People of ANWR a. Gwichin b. Inupiat	13a. Find the characteristics of the Gwichin tribe through a list.	14a. Describe how the Gwichin tribe utilizes the caribou through a flow chart.	15a. Use key cultural traits of the Gwichin people to share our results through a demonstration.	16a. Compare and contrast life cycles of the Gwichin and Inupiat through a song.	17a. Predict how the Inupiats will help the Gwichin adapt to drilling through a class discussion.	18a. Decide the value of each tribe's decision through an infomercial.
4. Government Response to ANWR a. local b. state c. federal	19a. Discover local laws affecting ANWR through a chart.	20a. Paraphrase the different government responses to ANWR through a class web.	21a. Summarize the local government's response to ANWR through a brochure.	22a. Analyze the views of BP, tribal leaders, and/or government leaders through a written report.	23a. Create a bill to present to the state legislature to protect ANWR through a mock legislative session.	24a. Assess the environmental impact of the government's responses to ANWR through a panel discussion.
5. Global Impact of Oil Drilling a. economic b. environmental	25a. Restate the factual content of ANWR through a test.	26a. Clarify the global impact of oil drilling in ANWR on the economy through a research paper.	27a. Categorize the environmental and economic concerns of ANWR through a Venn diagram.	28a. Determine the interrelationships in ANWR through a newspaper article.	29a. Create roles for a town meeting depicting ANWR personalities through a town meeting.	30a. Evaluate the global impact of oil drilling in ANWR through a town meeting.

Figure 5.7. Example of a Curry/Samara matrix

Note. From *CSM Unit Matrix*, by E. Alexander, M. Lee, K. Pahys, edited by The Curriculum Project. Retrieved May 16, 2005 from http://www.curriculumproject.com/cgi-bin/tcp_uw_matrix.cgi?unit=5&matrixType=6&agency=Cleveland+Heights-University+Heights+School+District&href=www.chuh.org&uw=true&sw=true. Copyright ©1985–2002 by J. Curry and J. Samara. Reprinted with permission.

Multiple Intelligences

Though never designed as a curricular model, Howard Gardner's (1983) theory of multiple intelligences provides a provocative and useful set of pathways to learning for students and teachers. Each intelligence is potentially an area of student talent or interest that can be considered when doing certain kinds of curricular planning. Gardner's nine intelligences (originally there were only seven) are:

- verbal-linguistic—the ability to use words and language effectively (writers, poets, journalists, orators, actors);
- spatial—the ability to perceive the visual/spatial world accurately and to change those perceptions (artists, inventors, decorators, architects);
- logical-mathematical—the ability to use numbers and logic effectively (scientists, tax accountants, mathematicians, computer programmers);
- interpersonal—the ability to perceive and understand intentions, motivations, and feelings of other people and the ability to respond to these;
- intrapersonal—the ability to understand one's self (moods, motivations, desires) and act on this knowledge to build self-discipline, understanding, and esteem;
- bodily/kinesthetic—facility in using one's hands and body to create things, as well as express ideas and feelings (mime, athlete, dancer, craftsperson, mechanic, surgeon);
- naturalist—understanding, recognition, and classification of the elements of one's surroundings, including the flora and fauna and other natural phenomena;
- musical—the ability to perceive, change, and communicate musical forms (music critic, composer, performer); and
- existential (still under consideration)—sensitivity to forces greater than one's self; interest in questions of the

significance of life and the meaning of death, the supernatural, and religion (theologians, philosophers, artists, physicists, clergy).

Unfortunately, this approach to intelligence has been misused to substitute for gifted programs and programming, and it has also been oversimplified to serve as a lesson plan template, which was never its intention. It was also not designed to replace traditional definitions of intelligence. It does, however, certainly fuel significant discussion about expanding definitions beyond a single test score and offers an alternative view of domains of human strengths and talent. Broader definitions are supported by Sternberg, Naglieri, Renzulli, and others, and the repercussions of expanded definitions of intelligence and talent are rippling through gifted education.

Gardner's multiple intelligences is *not* a list of components that need to be in every lesson or teaching/learning experience. Rather, they are best used as prompts for consideration in designing instructional units, particularly as they apply to student assessment and products of learning. For example, when using student contracts, students pursue independent investigations that extend learning or select from products that draw on the multiple intelligences to demonstrate their learning. When used in this manner, gifted students experience both the challenge and the choice essential to appropriate middle school curriculum.

The incorporation of interpersonal and intrapersonal experiences encourages students to make the necessary adolescent social and self-connections that are motivating and make learning meaningful. Teachers can and should on occasion require certain specific products (e.g., research papers) or projects (e.g., a science project trifold for poster sessions) in order to ensure that standards are demonstrated or, because in their professional judgments, certain materials or experiences are necessary for everyone. For more information on this topic, consider reading *Multiple Intelligences in the Classroom* (Armstrong, 2000) or visiting the

Web site for Gardner's Project Zero at http://pzweb.harvard.edu/Research/ResearchMI.htm.

Interdisciplinary Curricula

Both middle school advocates and gifted educators encourage the use of interdisciplinary curricula and units that allow students to make relevant connections among the disciplines and to themselves. Students explore themes and perspectives and develop skills that inform their lives in the present moment, as well as create a foundation for future study and experiences. Standards can be embedded in these units, as can study skills.

The frequency and organization of interdisciplinary units often reflect a school's schedule and the makeup of the interdisciplinary teaching team at a particular grade level. A two-person language arts/social studies team with a two-period block of time and common planning for teachers lends itself easily to coherent humanities unit development—a "fusion" approach (Vars, 1987) focused on broad themes such as "Man and Nature" or "Changes" that seamlessly blend study of multiple disciplines. A three-person language arts/social studies/science team without a common teaching block may have correlated content teaching without actual interdisciplinary units (Vars). With correlated content, for example, the English teacher might do nature poetry when the science teacher is covering botany and the social studies teacher reviews environmental legislation. But, the actual connections among these are often left for the students to make themselves unless teachers deliberately plan activities to structure their thinking process. The more common four-person team (language arts, social studies, science, and math) with common planning, but no block of student time may find interdisciplinary unit development impossible (or at least daunting) partly because of outside demands related to standards and testing. In this structure, teachers may revert to the "junior high school" departmental mindset. The following observation by Alexander and

George (1981) seems to be as true today as it was several decades ago:

> Thematic interdisciplinary units appear more or less frequently in almost all good middle school programs. However few, if any, middle schools (no matter how exemplary) seem to be able to sustain the use of thematic units as the curriculum of the basic instructional program for a majority of the day over a long period of several years or more. (p. 121)

Well-designed interdisciplinary studies for gifted students are supported by Clark (2002), Jacobs and Borland (1986), and Tomlinson et al. (2002). Because of gifted students' precocious abilities to discover analogies, parallels, contradictions, and contrasts in areas where their typical peers may see just the obvious, an interdisciplinary approach provides them a broader canvas for exploration and integration. As Maker (1982) stated, "the major focus of discussions, presentations, reading material and lectures in a gifted program should be on abstract concepts and generalizations that . . . transfer both within and across disciplines or fields of study" (p. 3). The danger in practice, however, is that interdisciplinary connections will be too narrowly demonstrated through culminating activities such as feasts, fairs, and showcases without the necessary content depth and complexity.

Interdisciplinary units can also be the foundation of self-contained gifted programming, accelerating grade-level challenge in content and pace. For example, a unit on "Law and Society" taught in either a pull-out or self-contained setting can include literature (e.g., *Nothing But the Truth*, *Inherit the Wind*, *To Kill a Mockingbird*, *Lord of the Flies*), mock trials and simulations, independent investigations, visits to courts and law schools, interviews with lawyers and other legal professionals, and the study of the impact of laws on science and vice versa, as well as the typical study of international, national, state, and local governments. The driving force would be abstract essential questions such as "Why do societies have laws?" Such an interdisciplinary unit also lends itself to problem solving at the school or community level. Thus, natural real-world connections would be made among three core content areas while addressing key components of good gifted curriculum and good curriculum for early adolescents. A variety of grade-level standards in multiple content areas could be embedded. Students would also have opportunities to explore themselves: their values, behaviors, and feelings. This unit could be taught to sixth- or seventh-grade gifted students in a 10-week quarter. The pace, reading level, and focus on abstract concepts and connections are what distinguish it from what might be offered to typical middle school students. Figure 5.8 also provides a sample plan for an interdisciplinary unit that combines standards and activities from content areas with typical district-level gifted standards.

Many middle schools "house" the focus of their gifted program in a reading or English class because the communication arts (reading, writing, listening, speaking, viewing) lend themselves so easily to integrated or interdisciplinary instruction. Themes or topics from any area of study can incorporate these language arts areas and their national, state, and local standards.

Strategies: The "How to" of Teaching and Learning

While several of the strategies described below can and should be used with all middle school students, they are particularly valuable for gifted students because of their emphasis on higher level abstract thinking. While all students should have access to higher level thinking activities, they should make up the largest portion of a gifted student's classroom experiences and activities since the basic content and skills should have already been mastered. A preassessment is essential, however, to confirm this level of achievement. Teachers should not just depend on

Part of a Sample Unit Plan		
Language Arts	Social Studies	Gifted
Goals: 1. Increase ability to analyze character in a novel. 2. Understand role of setting influencing plot and character. 3. Develop appreciation for Native American legend and folklore.	**Goals:** 1. Locate major North American Indian tribes on a map. 2. Understand differing cultures of major American Indian tribes. 3. Trace history of treatment of Indians in North America.	**Goals:** 1. Demonstrate understanding of varying social organizational structures. 2. Demonstrate behavior that shows compassion for and understanding of individual differences and cultural diversity. 3. Demonstrate ability to work with others in large- and small-group activities.
Activities: 1. Read *A Light in the Forest* from the Indian literature anthology. 2. Write character analysis of Uncle Wilse, True Son, or the Reverend, explaining how the setting affected him. 3. Attend Indian storytelling at the Cleveland Museum of Art and view the Indian exhibit.	**Activities:** 1. Text reading 2. Map 3. Simulation: Collision	**Activities:** 1. Make a chart comparing the social organizations of two different tribes. 2. Journal writing 3. *Learning Discussion Skills Through Games* activities

Figure 5.8. Sample planning matrix used for developing a fused language arts/social studies unit on Native Americans for middle grades gifted students

Note. From "Making Connections: Integrative Curriculum and the Gifted," by G. Vars and S. Rakow, 1993, *Roeper Review, 16,* p. 52. Copyright ©1993 by the Roeper Institute. Reprinted with permission.

general standardized test scores for assumptions about unit-specific knowledge and skills. (More specific information on pre-assessment can be found in Chapter 6.)

Socratic Seminars

Socrates believed that dialogue was the essential component for learning. Socratic seminars, popularized at least in part as a result of Mortimer J. Adler's *The Paideia Proposal* (1982), *Paideia Problems and Possibilities* (1983), and *The Paideia Program* (1984), are designed to engage students in high-level dialogue about a complex text or artifact. It differs from Socratic questioning in that, after the initial opening or core question, the dialogue is guided by the participants themselves. Socratic seminars can be used in any content area. Because they actively involve students with the material, they can serve as authentic performance assessments when used with appropriate rubrics.

The seminar depends upon close reading and study and everyone's active participation. This participation is initiated by a challenging opening question that is selected because it has no right, wrong, or quick and easy answer. The discussion is facilitated by a seminar leader who is also a participant. Initially, the teacher would be the seminar leader so that he or she could model appropriate questioning, clarifications, and reflective thinking. However, the eventual goal is for the students to take over the leadership role. When students are serving as leaders, the teacher becomes just another equal participant.

The emphasis of a seminar is on deep understanding of the ideas, perspectives, and ambiguity inherent in an important text, not memorization of information. If used in a more heterogeneous setting, classroom teachers might pose the same core or opening question, but have the students prepare for the seminar using multiple texts at various reading levels. In that case, the learning outcomes would be focused more on addressing the question than on the reading of a single text.

Copeland (2005) provides excellent guidelines for using "Socratic Circles" in middle school, including specific directions for establishing seminars, text suggestions, curricular alignment, assessment and follow-up activities, questioning strategies, and interpersonal dynamics. A video by the Association for Supervision and Curriculum Development (1999) also shows a seminar in action.

Simulations and Role-Playing

Simulations provide opportunities for experiential learning in real-world situations and are based on constructivist principles. They are midway between a game and an unstructured role-play. Simulations use compressed time to provide a "slice of life." Good simulations integrate curriculum, authentic assessment, and engaged learning. The teacher plays the role of facilitator during a simulation and has the responsibility of carefully assigning roles if the model includes this. In addition, he or she manages the materials and resources available to students.

In the humanities, simulations can provide opportunities for empathy and understanding of other people, places, and times as students take on a variety of identities. In math and the sciences, they allow students the opportunity to see the "unseen" through computer modeling and experiment with the consequences of individual and group decisions on the "unthinkable"—wars, natural disasters, plagues. Students play roles, solve problems, make decisions, and experience the consequences of those decisions as individuals, a whole class, or in small groups. In many simulations, students have the opportunity to do research, practice public speaking, collaborate with classmates, and write and create visual aids.

Simulations can be created by the teacher (see Kraft & Martin, 1993, for steps in designing a simulation) or purchased (many excellent simulations are available for a reasonable cost from Interact, http://www.teachinteract.com). They can be paper-based (like a court-trial), Web-based (like a stock market simulation), or computer-based (like an interactive brain surgery program). Digital technologies have expanded the possibilities for simulations into every area of learning, and simulations are often used in training adults in business, medicine, and other professions.

Key components of a simulation are the underlying concepts and information, teamwork and interpersonal skills used during the activity, and the debriefing, in which students describe what they experienced and what happened, analyze and connect their experiences, and contemplate how they can apply and extend their learning. This last component is critical to lasting learning. Without debriefing, students may believe that the simulation was just another "fun" or "cool" activity. The teacher's role in facilitating concept development and learning at the conclusion of the simulation is essential.

Again, the advantage of this approach for gifted students is the opportunity to apply advanced knowledge to problem-solving situations. Simulations often unveil the complexity of issues and situations. When purchasing simulations for gifted middle school students, teachers can often use high-school-level materials because of students' advanced reading comprehension, abstract thinking and cognitive sophistication, or content mastery. When a simulation is used in a heterogeneous setting, teachers can vary students' roles and select a range of resources to ensure that all students engage with the content and problem solving at appropriately advanced levels.

For all middle school students, simulations and role-playing teach necessary and important lessons in interpersonal skills and relationships. In my experience, students remembered their simulation experiences years after they had left my class. The roles they played, the dilemmas they faced, and the interactions they had with others in the class provided both cognitive and affective learning opportunities that had a lasting influence.

Problem-Based Learning (PBL)
and Creative Problem Solving (CPS)

Because of the nature of gifted students to question and probe the "gray areas" and ambiguities of knowledge and ideas, problem-based learning (PBL) and Creative Problem Solving (CPS) are excellent instructional strategies.

Problem-based learning organizes content and curriculum around carefully structured "fuzzy" problems. The teacher selects and develops the problem, matching the skills and content required to solve it to the curriculum and standards. In addition, a well-chosen problem makes a connection between the content and the students' lives, interests, and concerns. Usually in groups, students apply multiple research, reasoning, and interpersonal skills to gather interdisciplinary knowledge and create solutions.

Teachers act as coaches and facilitators as students go through four stages: (1) clarifying and defining the problem; (2) gathering, evaluating, and using information; (3) developing and evaluating possible solutions; and (4) creatively presenting the best one to a significant audience. "Problem-based learning enables students to embrace complexity, find relevance and joy in their learning, and enhance their capacity for creative and responsible real-world problem solving" (Illinois Math and Science Academy, 2005, ¶ 1). Increasingly, colleges and medical and professional schools are embracing this model of instruction.

Creative Problem Solving is a similar model. Designed by Sidney Parnes, CPS is a highly structured method for problem solving that emphasizes the creative processes involved in developing multiple alternatives before selecting solutions. The process encourages students to accept the "messy" nature of problems and work through a series of sequential steps to describe the "mess," clarify the problem, find relevant data, freely and nonjudgmentally generate multiple ideas to solve the problem, design and apply evaluation criteria for the possible solutions, and finally select the best solution. Students then design and produce a plan to "sell" the solution to relevant stakeholders who should take action on the solution.

As with PBL, CPS can be used in any content area, in an advisory, or in an interdisciplinary curriculum. It is particularly appropriate for gifted students because it approximates the role of scholars in different disciplines while cultivating both divergent and convergent thinking skills. Students work in collaborative groups that benefit from both individual expertise and cooperation (Maker & Nielson, 1995).

For more information, try *Creative Problem Solving for Teens* (Elwell, 1993). In addition, the Future Problem Solving (http://www.fpsp.org) and Odyssey of the Mind (http://www.odyssey ofthemind.com) programs incorporate CPS techniques.

Independent Study and Learning Contracts

Sometimes, the most valuable choice teachers can provide for individuals or small groups of students is through independent study and learning contracts. These allow students to extend their learning by providing them the opportunity to connect classroom content with personal interests or to explore new questions initiated by classroom study. Learning contracts keep students accountable for both time and content, and they balance requirements set by the teacher with alternative activities designed or selected jointly by teacher and student. Contracts can guide independent study for an individual student or be used with a whole class to broaden students' choices for activities and assessments.

The Menu Model is one way to apply contracts. Students are provided with a menu of activities that address the standards, essential questions, and content. This menu can be interdisciplinary, or it can reflect multiple intelligences or just aspects of a particular concept. Figure 5.9 contains a sample menu and contract I created for use in a seventh-grade gifted class that combined language arts and history.

Menu of Civil War Explorations

Introduction and Expectations:

The Civil War was a devastating experience for our young country. We have skimmed the surface of the issues and events involved. To get a deeper understanding of the causes, events, and consequences surrounding the war, you will participate in a variety of explorations of the topic. Everyone will complete a total of 150 points selected from four categories: historical fiction, maps, creative arts, and biography. Please read over the descriptions and complete the contract to let me know which activities you have chosen. Rubrics are attached explaining the assessment criteria in each category.

In any category, if you have a different idea, you are welcome to suggest alternatives that you can present to me for discussion. Together, we'll create an assessment rubric and assign a point value.

50 points
  I. Historical Fiction
  <u>All students must read</u> *Across Five Aprils* and complete the novel packet. (Alternative titles may be substituted after a conference with me.)

15 points
  II. Map Assignment
  A. Make a map of <u>key</u> Civil War battles including who won them.
  B. Make a map showing the Union states and the Confederate states.
  C. Make a map showing Sherman's march to the sea.
  D. Other ideas?

20 points
  III. Creative Arts Assignment
  A. Act out part of *Uncle Tom's Cabin* by Harriet Beecher Stowe.
  B. Perform an interpretive reading of *Up From Slavery* by Booker T. Washington
  C. Draw the uniforms of the Union and the Confederate armies.

continued on next page

Figure 5.9. Sample menu and contract

Curricular and Instructional Strategies   **129**

D. Listen to a collection of songs of the war era. What do they reveal about the country, the people, and the culture of that time? How do they fit with American folk/roots music traditions? What else can you tell about this music?

E. The American Civil War was the first major war to be thoroughly photographed. Especially noteworthy are the pictures of the pioneer photographer Matthew Brady. Get a pictorial history of the Civil War. Study the photographs and then write your reactions to them. Do these photographs suggest that war is a glorious adventure or do they portray the grim reality of war? Why? Respond to the photographs in an essay, poem, picture, or song of your own creation.

F. Other ideas?

25 points

IV. Biography Project

A. Write a one-page obituary for someone from this era, highlighting his/her contributions to America and why we, as a nation, should mourn his/her loss.

B. Write a dialogue between Booker T. Washington and W. E. B. DuBois exposing the differences in their views about how African-Americans should behave and what paths they should take to succeed in America.

C. Who was Dred Scott? How did the Dred Scott decision reflect the values and conflicts of the time?

D. Compare and contrast Grant's military leadership with Lee's.

E. What were women's contributions during this time period and during the war? Cite those of both ordinary and famous women of the time.

F. Other ideas?

40 points

V. Miscellaneous

Choose from the attached list or do additional projects from the lists above. You may also propose additional ideas. Use this opportunity to address questions you have about the events of the war, its causes, its aftermath, the people involved, or anything else that interests you. You might also consider comparing the American Civil War to other civil wars that have occurred in other nations in the world.

Contract for Civil War Explorations

Name: _____

I will complete the explorations as stated below. If I run into problems, I will ask for help. I will use a variety of sources, use effective time management skills, bring the materials I need to class, and work well with others in the class. I will follow the class rules whether I am working alone or with a group.

I. Historical Fiction (50 points)
_____ I will read *Across Five Aprils* and complete the packet.
_____ I will read _____ and complete the packet.

II. Map Assignment (15 points)
I will complete Map assignment (circle one) A   B   C
I will complete the following Map assignment that I have designed and discussed with my teacher:

III. Creative Arts Assignment (20 points)
I will complete Creative Arts assignment (circle one) A B C D E
I will complete the following Creative Arts assignment that I have designed and discussed with my teacher:

IV. Biography Project (25 points)
I will complete Biography Project A   B   C   D   E
I will complete the following Biography Project that I have designed and discussed with my teacher:

V. Miscellaneous (40 points)
I will do the following activities selected from the assignment sheet or that I have designed and discussed with my teacher:

Teacher Signature: _____

Student Signature: _____

Parent Signature: _____

Mastery Learning

Mastery learning is an instructional process created by Benjamin Bloom based on the learning theory of John B. Carroll and popularized by Thomas Guskey (1996). While primarily designed to offer expanded opportunities to learn for those with a slower rate of learning or those who lack prerequisite skills, it also offers potential for students with a more rapid learning pace and extensive prior knowledge. Following a pretest (or "formative assessment") on the target objective, students are divided into two groups: those with mastery (or with prerequisite skills) and those without. Those with mastery move on to what Guskey calls "Enrichment Activities." Those without mastery participate in instructional activities (for the first unit or skill in a sequence), or "Correctives," for subsequent units. These short instructional cycles and use of flexible short-term groupings limit negative effects of labeling for either high achievers or struggling students. It provides opportunities for teachers to document mastery of standards and allows gifted students the opportunity to advance.

Guskey (1996) defined *enrichment* as opportunities for students that expand or broaden their learning through involvement in topics of their choice. He reiterated the importance of ensuring that enrichment is not busywork:

> We must recognize that students involved in enrichment activities also have special learning needs. Furthermore, involving these fast learners in busywork just to keep them occupied is detrimental to their learning progress. High-quality enrichment activities are essential to these students' learning and to the mastery learning process. (p. 119)

Thus, enrichment activities must have two essential characteristics: They must be (a) rewarding to students and (b) challenging, valuable learning experiences. They can be in the same content area or in a different area of interest to the student. Use of enrichment activities is a particularly useful approach in a heterogeneous setting when the objective or outcome is mastery of specific skills or information. For example,

- grammar skills mini-lessons;
- map skills and mapping;
- science labeling (e.g., solar system, parts of a cell, steps in mitosis);
- vocabulary (in any content area);
- fractions (addition, subtraction, multiplication, division, application in word problems);
- computer skills (designing a Web page, creating a PowerPoint presentation, basic word processing); and
- measurement.

Guskey (1996) noted, however, that use of mastery learning in heterogeneous classrooms is not a substitute for special education or gifted education, but rather a complement to them.

Curriculum Compacting

Like mastery learning, curriculum compacting (Reis, Burns, & Renzulli, 1992) provides opportunities for students to test out of material and "buy time" for curricular extensions, advanced material, or independent study. Curriculum compacting is designed to allow students to move through the regular curriculum at a faster pace, and it is especially appropriate in a text-based course or unit, when bright students may know more than 75% of the material in the text. This is particularly true since many basal texts have been "dumbed down" two grade levels over recent years (Reis, Burns, & Renzulli).

There are eight parts to the process of curriculum compacting:

1. Identify the relevant learning objectives in a subject area or grade level.
2. Find or create ways to pretest students on these objectives.
3. Identify students who may benefit from curriculum compacting.
4. Administer the pretest to uncover existing achievement levels.
5. Eliminate drill-and-practice activities for those who have mastery.
6. Provide "streamlined" instruction at a rapid pace to "fill in" those objectives not yet mastered.
7. Offer opportunities for enrichment or acceleration for students whose curriculum has been compacted, including advanced interdisciplinary extensions, connections, and projects.
8. Keep records of the process and options available to "compacted" students. (Reis, Burns, & Renzulli, 1992, p. 8)

Gifted students are first assessed for mastery of the relevant goals and objectives of the regular curriculum and standards. This provides diagnostic information for the teacher. In most cases, it is not necessary to test the whole class. This could be a disincentive to learning for struggling students. Rather, the teacher should use his or her judgment to determine which students should take the test on particular objectives. In some cases, however, giving the pretest might be part of helping all students to set learning goals and take responsibility for their own progress. As in many aspects of teaching, there's no definitive answer here. Teacher judgment is the key.

When appropriate, more challenging opportunities are provided to students who "test out." Records are kept of the diagnostic test, as well as student work products during the time they have "bought" for enrichment, acceleration, and investigation of related topics beyond the typical curriculum. For middle school students for whom good time management and independent work habits may still be goals, work logs may also be kept to ensure that this time is used productively.

Teacher support and monitoring are essential here because content mastery or giftedness is no guarantee that a middle school student has the maturity to work independently and productively for an extended period of time. In addition, students may need guidance in selecting topics, projects, and resources. It is important that the gifted student not feel abandoned while allowed to progress at a faster pace or into deeper material. Time for one-to-one or small-group conferencing with the teacher should be built into the design when this approach is used.

What About Direct Instruction?

It might be easy to assume from the list above that direct instruction is not recommended for gifted students. Obviously, this is not the case. When it is clear that a gifted student or group of students lacks knowledge or skill mastery, then direct instruction can be an important tool.

There are two key components, however, to determining this strategy's effectiveness with a gifted population: preassessment (to ensure and demonstrate that students really don't know the material) and a rapid pace of presentation. Typically, gifted students master new material more quickly and can progress through content faster than their age peers. A single presentation is often all that is necessary, rather than the repetitions in multiple modalities that might characterize instruction in a heterogeneous class of typical middle school students. In addition, there should be adequate opportunity for student questions and extending the conceptual depth and complexity of the material where appropriate. Particularly in homogeneous advanced classes, direct instruction should be modified for gifted students.

Conclusion

It may seem overwhelming to anyone working on curricular design and instructional planning to consider all of these choices. Our approach must be knowledgeable, but eclectic. In a single school, a student may be enrolled in a pre-AP math class (because AP math is offered at the high school); a heterogeneous social studies class that uses Socratic seminars, as well as problem-based and mastery learning techniques; a computer skills class that uses curriculum compacting; and a language arts class for superior cognitive gifted students that is built on interdisciplinary units and uses menus and contracts.

Masterful teaching is an art. Planning curricula and choosing instruction are like selecting and combining paint colors from an almost unlimited palette. Ultimately, the outcome is the result of interaction among the creative process, the artist's skills, and the viewer in the same way that learning outcomes are the result of the planning and selection process, the teacher's skills, and the learner.

Next Steps . . . Taking Action

1. Examine existing state and local middle grades and high school standards, as well as those of NAGC and national discipline organizations such as the National Council of Teachers of English (NCTE) and the National Council of Teachers of Mathematics (NCTM).

2. Examine existing school curricula and identify areas where changes are needed to meet the needs of gifted students.

3. Identify strategies that would be appropriate for your students, classes, school, and community, choosing from those described in this chapter or others.

4. Work with colleagues to design appropriate curricular units and extension activities, choosing from those described in this chapter or others.

5. Communicate changes in curricular and instructional techniques to administrators, colleagues, and parents.

6. Arrange adequate funding for resources if necessary.

7. Work with colleagues in study groups to understand, implement, and assess new units and strategies. Be sure to look at student achievement and work samples to help determine success.

8. Make ongoing revisions to respond to current research and changing student needs.

References

Adler, M. J. (1982). *The Paideia proposal: An educational manifesto.* New York: Macmillan.

Adler, M. J. (1983). *Paideia problems and possibilities: A consideration of questions raised by the Paideia Proposal.* New York: Macmillan.

Adler, M. J. (1984). *The Paideia program: An educational syllabus.* New York: Macmillan.

Alexander, W. M., & George, P. S. (1981). *The exemplary middle school.* New York: CBS College Publishing.

Anderson, L. W., & Krathwohl, D. R. (Eds). (2001). *A taxonomy for learning, teaching, and assessment: A revision of Bloom's Taxonomy of Educational Objectives.* New York: Longman.

Anfara, V. A. (2004). Creating high-performance middle schools: Recommendations from research. In S. C. Thompson (Ed.), *Reforming middle level education: Considerations for policymakers* (pp. 1–18). Greenwich, CT: Information Age.

Armstrong, T. (2000). *Multiple intelligences in the classroom* (2nd ed.). Alexandria, VA: Association for Supervision and Curriculum Development.

Association for Supervision and Curriculum Development (ASCD). (1999). *How to conduct successful Socratic seminars: A video series for the classroom teacher.* Alexandria, VA: Author.

Beane, J. A. (1990). *A middle school curriculum: From rhetoric to reality.* Columbus, OH: National Middle School Association.

Beane, J. (2004). Creating quality in middle school curriculum. In S. C. Thompson (Ed.), *Reforming middle level education: Considerations for policymakers* (pp. 49–63). Greenwich, CT: Information Age.

Betts, G., & Kercher, J. (1999). *Autonomous Learner Model: Optimizing ability.* Greeley, CO: Autonomous Learning Publications & Specialists.

Bloom, B. S. (Ed.). (1956). *Taxonomy of educational objectives: The classification of educational goals. Handbook 1: Cognitive domain.* White Plains, NY: Longman.

Clark, B. (2002). *Growing up gifted: Developing the potential of children at home and at school* (6th ed.). Upper Saddle River, NJ: Merrill/Prentice Hall.

Copeland, M. (2005). *Socratic circles: Fostering critical and creative thinking in middle and high school.* Portland, ME: Stenhouse.

Cruz, E. (2002). Bloom's revised taxonomy. *Encyclopedia of Educational Technology.* Retrieved May 12, 2005, from http://coe.sdsu.edu/eet/Articles/bloomrev/index.htm

Elwell, P. (1993). *Creative problem solving for teens.* Waco, TX: Prufrock Press.

Erb, T. O. (Ed.). (2001). *This we believe . . . and now we must act.* Westerville, OH: National Middle School Association.

Gardner, H. (1983). *Frames of mind: The theory of multiple intelligences.* New York: BasicBooks.

George, P. S. (1997). A second look at grouping, the gifted, and middle school education. In T. O. Erb (Ed.), *Dilemmas in talent development in the middle grades: Two views* (pp. 113–145). Westerville, OH: National Middle School Association.

Guskey, T. R. (1996). *Implementing mastery learning* (2nd ed.). Belmont, CA: Wadsworth.

Illinois Math and Science Academy (2005). *PBLN @ IMSA overview.* Retrieved May 12, 2005, from http://www2.imsa.edu/programs/pbln/overview/mission.php

Jackson, A. W., & Davis, G. A. (2000). *Turning points 2000: Educating adolescents in the 21st century.* New York: Teachers College Press.

Kraft, K., & Martin, P. (1993). Coming to America: A simulation based on the Ellis Island experience. *The Prufrock Journal, 4*(3), 14–17.

Krathwohl, D., Bloom, B., & Masia, B. (1964). *Taxonomy of educational objectives: The classification of educational goals. Handbook II: The affective domain.* New York: MacKay.

Jacobs, H. H., & Borland, J. H. (1986). The interdisciplinary concept model: Theory and practice. *Gifted Child Quarterly, 30,* 159–163.

Lounsbury, J., & Vars, G. (1978). *A curriculum for the middle school years.* Columbus, OH: Merrill.

Maker, C. J. (1982). *Teaching models in the education of the gifted.* Rockville, MD: Aspen Systems.

Maker, C. J., & Nielson, A. B. (1995). *Teaching models in the education of the gifted* (2nd ed.). Austin, TX: PRO-ED.

National Middle School Association. (2003). *This we believe: Successful schools for young adolescents.* Columbus, OH: Author.

Reis, S. M., Burns, D. E., & Renzulli, J. S. (1992). *Curriculum compacting: The complete guide to modifying the regular curriculum for high ability students*. Mansfield Center, CT: Creative Learning Press.

Renzulli, J. S. (2000). Part I: One way to organize exploratory curriculum: Academies of inquiry and talent development. *Middle School Journal, 32*(2), 5–14. Retrieved May 12, 2005, from http://www.sp.uconn.edu/~nrcgt/pdf/aitdp1.pdf

Renzulli, J. S. (2001). Part II: Academies of inquiry and talent development. *Middle School Journal, 32*(3), 7–14. Retrieved May 12, 2005, from http://www.sp.uconn.edu/~nrcgt/pdf/aitdp2.pdf

Renzulli, J. S., & Reis, S. M. (1997). Giftedness in middle school students: A talent development perspective. In T. O. Erb (Ed.), *Dilemmas in talent development in the middle grades: Two views* (pp. 43–112). Westerville, OH: National Middle School Association.

Stevenson, C. (2001). Curriculum that is challenging, integrative, and exploratory. In T. O. Erb, (Ed.) *This we believe . . . and now we must act* (pp. 63-68). Westerville, OH: National Middle School Association.

Tomlinson, C. A., Kaplan, S. N., Renzulli, J. S., Purcell, J., Leppien, J., & Burns, D. (2002). *The parallel curriculum: A design to develop high potential and challenge high-ability learners*. Thousand Oaks, CA: Corwin Press.

Vars, G. F. (1987). *Interdisciplinary teaching in the middle grades*. Columbus, OH: National Middle School Association.

Williamson, R. D., and Johnston, J. H. (2004). Creating academically challenging middle level schools for every child. In S. C. Thompson (Ed.), *Reforming middle level education: Considerations for policymakers* (pp. 33–48). Greenwich, CT: Information Age.

Wiggins, G., & McTighe, J. (1998). *Understanding by design*. Alexandria, VA: Association for Supervision and Curriculum Development.

Differentiating Instruction: Supplement to, Not Substitute for, Gifted Programming

Essential Questions

1. What is differentiation?

2. How can differentiated instruction and curricula be used in a variety of middle school settings to meet the needs of gifted students?

Differentiation of instruction is such a significant component of good middle school education and good gifted education that it needs and deserves its own chapter. While some strategies discussed in the previous chapter will certainly play a role in a differentiated classroom, there is a lot more to consider.

What is Differentiation?

"Differentiated instruction" is a popular current focus for staff development. It is particularly popular in middle school circles because it fits so comfortably with heterogeneous grouping. The National Middle School Association officially endorses differen-

tiated approaches (e.g., independent study, enrichment programs). *This We Believe . . . And Now We Must Act* (Erb, 2003),
NMSA's position statement on middle school education, supports
differentiation as "practices that respond to the variety of student
competencies, interests, and abilities and meet the needs of
advanced learners" (p. 30).

While not a substitute for advanced classes and other elements of a continuum of services for meeting gifted students'
needs, differentiation can be a useful approach to middle school
students' wide range of interests, abilities, and learning styles. A
differentiated approach to teaching and learning can apply in
both outwardly homogeneous gifted classes and heterogeneous
classes (in which the differences are just more obvious!).

Differentiating curricula and instruction for varied learners is
not new, perhaps dating back to the one-room schoolhouse.
Certainly though, in the 1960s and 1970s, a similarly intentioned
approach was popular under the terms "individualized instruction" (II) or "individually prescribed instruction" (IPI). Based on
the acceptance of the idea that pupils differ and recognition that
these differences must be provided for, Clark Lingren's (1970)
description of IPI included many of the elements of today's differentiated instruction model: preassessment, individual assignments, teacher instruction or coaching, and postassessment for
mastery (Vars, 2003). At that time, however, there was a narrower
range of student diversity in general education, and even with
that, implementation for more than 25 students was nearly
impossible. Tomlinson (2001) supports the direction and intention of individualized instruction. But, she points out that today's
differentiated instruction uses a greater balance of individual,
whole-class, and small-group instruction, as well as broader curricular themes and topics, instead of the fragmented learning that
often occurred in individualized instruction.

Some of the earliest roots of differentiated instruction in the
field of gifted education were expressed by Virgil Ward. His 1980
book, *Differential Education for the Gifted* (formerly a 1961 volume

entitled *Education for the Gifted: An Axiomatic Approach*) laid out both the argument for and a process to develop differentiated curricula for gifted students. His definition went back even further to the 1959 *Dictionary of Education* in which *differentiation* was defined as " a plan for meeting individual differences; the content of instruction may differ in degree of difficulty, areas of student interest, quantity and quality of content, or context" (cited in Ward, 1980, p. xliv). Working definitions today are not significantly different from this. Under other names, special educators involved in "mainstreaming" (1970s–80s) and "inclusion" (1990s–2000s) have also been historical advocates for this approach. But, what is new is the broader reliance on differentiation to meet the needs of ever-widening ability ranges in general education classrooms.

Carol Ann Tomlinson, the most recent voice for differentiated instruction, taught middle school gifted students for more than 20 years. Before her more generalized publications on differentiation, her ideas were developed to help meet the needs of gifted students, particularly when they were in general education classes. She has defined differentiation as "a systematic approach to planning curriculum and instruction for academically diverse learners" (Tomlinson & Eidson, 2003, p. 3).

One of the most common misconceptions is the idea that differentiation is a single strategy or even one set of strategies. In actuality, any strategy could be part of implementing the key philosophical premise behind differentiation: instruction should begin with the students. This is also a key principle of middle school education. Without first identifying and understanding the needs of our students, as individuals and as subgroups, real differentiation cannot occur.

However, differentiation goes beyond student choice. There is *intentionality* behind how students select, are guided toward, or are assigned certain activities or projects. This is different from what is often seen in supposedly differentiated classrooms: students working on different projects in small groups or individually. From casual observation, however, it would be impossible to know. Using a gifted student's extraordinary research paper as evidence of differentiation would only show that connection if the teacher had intentionally structured some experiences that led the student to higher achievement. It's not enough that he or she just "did more" or even "did better" than his or her classmates or for teachers to just "have higher expectations."

Preassessment: Finding a Starting Point

Careful reading of the work of Tomlinson and others (e.g., Gregory & Chapman, 2001; Heacox, 2001; Winebrenner, 2001; Kingore, 2002, 2004) reveals that the first step in differentiation is gathering information on individual students in the areas of motivation, learning style, interest, ability/potential, and achievement. This includes a review of students' permanent folders or past test data and grades, as well as timely administration of specific content preassessments and inventories of interest, style, and motivation.

In middle schools, this information can be gathered efficiently through team collaboration. One teacher can administer an interest inventory, one a motivation instrument, and one a learning style inventory. Alternatively, these might all be completed and discussed during advisory periods and then shared with the team. Students, too, can be invited to participate in goal setting, instructional planning, and evaluating progress.

Individual content teachers are best suited to administering unit- or skill-specific preassessments. The gifted coordinator or building resource teacher should make sure that all teachers are aware of which students in their classes have been identified as gifted and in which areas, just as they are made aware of other special-needs students and their mandated accommodations. This will help address underachievement as caring teachers ask, "Jenny was identified as gifted in math, but I'm not seeing it in my Prealgebra class. I wonder why . . . ?"

As with special-education students, for whom the collection

of this information provides the basis of their IEP, this data should guide the creation of some form of written plan for gifted and talented students. The format for these vary by state or local district, or they can be created for use in a particular school. All information can be gathered in a student profile, which can be shared at team meetings and modified annually. Computers can make access to this information easy. This written plan and student profile provide the starting point for differentiation in each class. The sample in Figure 6.1 can be modified to fit the needs of each individual team or school setting.

Planning for Differentiation

Once teachers have the preassessment information, it can inform their decision making about instruction and how best to create the "magic" that occurs at the vital intersection of teacher, students, and content. This includes whether and how to use grouping, what materials and resources are necessary, what kinds of homework and research assignments will best enhance students' learning, and so on. This is also when teachers consider which (if any) of the commonly cited differentiation strategies are appropriate: tiered assignments, orbital studies, independent study, group investigations, learning centers, the Menu Model, and choice boards (e.g., "Tic Tac Toe" [Winebrenner, 2001]). The most commonly cited classroom elements that provide opportunities for differentiation are

- content (material being studied and the important concepts and knowledge being learned);
- product (how students will demonstrate their learning);
- process (how students engage with the topic, including varied multilevel materials, independent research, and direct instruction); and
- environment (how the classroom is arranged and flows).

Date: _____ Age: _____

Name: Jamie Doe

Standardized Test Scores

    Achievement
    Test Scores:
        Math   98%
        Reading   93%
        Science   98%
        Social Studies: 93%

    Cognitive Abilities
    Test Score: 99th percentile

Areas of Gifted
Identification: math, science,
                 superior cognitive ability

Grades: All A's and B's last year;
                 strongest areas are math
                 and science

Work Habits
and Learning Style: Poor organizational skills
                 Not a well-developed writer
                 Enjoys talking to adults
                 Prefers working alone; shuts
                 down when doing group projects

Interests: Loves computers and has great
                 skills
                 Excellent violinist

Specific Preassessment Data:

Figure 6.1. Student profile

Parents and administrators, as well as students, must be prepared for differentiation if it is to occur successfully. Just as they practice any of their other school routines and behaviors (getting water, sharpening pencils, fire drills), students need to practice working in small groups and independently, including how to get questions answered and what to do when they're "stuck." One suggestion is "Ask Three, Then Me," where students who have a question must ask three other students before the teacher. This way, students learn to work together before instantly interrupting the teacher at the first sign of confusion.

Students also need to get comfortable with classrooms in which everyone may be doing something different. Teachers need to be proactive in order to eliminate the constant early adolescent whine of "That's not fair!" The following "Band-Aid example" is a good place to start:

> Imagine, class, that Jill cuts her finger and comes to me for a Band-Aid. How would it be if I either told her, "No, I can't give you a Band-Aid because I'm not giving one to everyone in the class, so it wouldn't be fair," or if I said, "Okay," to Jill and then made everyone else put a Band-Aid on their finger, too. Of course, this is silly! Not everyone needs a Band-Aid right now. In our classroom, we try to have everyone get what he or she needs when he or she needs it.

Of course, this will take some practice before it becomes standard classroom procedure.

Teachers will also need to be sensitive to students' perceptions. For example, when using tiered assignments, teachers might put each level of activity on a different color assignment paper. If the most challenging work is always on blue and the least challenging always on yellow, students will quickly realize what it means to get the yellow sheet. But, if the colors rotate, students will stop wondering who has which assignment. This is also true for calling them Activity 1 and 2, A and B, and so forth. If teachers are using various flexible grouping methods (interest, learning style, achievement), students will not be labeled or always find themselves in a "bluebird" or "crow" group. This approach to grouping is supported by middle school advocates McEwin, Dickinson, and Jenkins (2003) based on the position of the national Forum to Accelerate Middle-Grades Reform: "When students are grouped and regrouped for instruction, the assignment should be 'temporary and based on diagnosed needs, interests, and talents of students, not on a single achievement test'" (p. 58).

An anchor activity is what students turn to when they are finished or, for some other reason, find themselves waiting for computer time, for the pass to the library, or for the teacher's attention (Tomlinson, 2001). These activities should be productive learning opportunities to which students learn to move automatically and independently. Obviously, with adolescents, this takes practice! Some possible anchor activities are reading, practicing with manipulatives, or reviewing vocabulary with flashcards. In some settings, each student could have an "Anchor Folder" in the classroom. Books or articles, math brainteasers or problems, flash cards, maps, instructional CDs and DVDs, directions for Webquests, and other individually significant work could be kept there and updated by the students, teachers, or both. In the beginning, it makes sense to practice for short periods of time with just two groups, one doing the anchor activities and one working with the teacher and then switching. This will help students get used to the process.

Standards (national, state, professional organization, etc.) are a useful tool in differentiating instruction. Above-grade-level standards can provide a guide for adding depth and complexity for gifted students, while below-grade-level standards can help fill in gaps for struggling learners. Demonstrated mastery of the standards on a preassessment "buys" students time for alternative learning experiences, especially during extended periods of state and local test preparation, skill practice, and review. This is often called "telescoping" or "curriculum compacting," terms that refer to eliminating work students have already mastered or streamlining work so that students can achieve mastery at a rate more compatible with their rapid learning pace (Reis, Burns, & Renzulli, 1992). With this extra time, more challenging content is substituted (see Chapter 5 for more details on curriculum compacting.)

Start Small

Differentiated Homework and Tiered Assignments

Differentiation can take many forms—from simple, small, short-term accommodations, to a whole school year of sequenced and fully differentiated units. One first step for teachers interested in trying out this approach is differentiated homework assignments. For example, Ms. Yelsky, a social studies teacher working with a heterogeneous class of students in a unit on elections, wanted her students to connect their learning about government to the current national, state, and local elections. Her students had a wide range of reading and thinking skills. She wanted everyone involved in discussions of the issues, but she wanted students to investigate issues that were of particular significance to them. Following initial exposure to the ideas of differentiation, she started with a small change in how she would have students do their current events projects. All students would find articles in newspapers and magazines, but she would *assign* Level I or Level II follow-up, as can be seen in Figure 6.2. Some things to notice in this assignment:

- All students engage in higher level thinking. The proportion of concrete to abstract is what differs.
- All students do the same amount of work—it's just different work. This is developmentally appropriate because of middle school students' sense of what's "fair."

Goals/Objectives: Reading Comprehension
                             Government/Elections
                             Summarizing

Level I—News Article Questions

Title of the Newspaper/Magazine: _____

Date of the Newspaper/Magazine: _____

Title and Author/Source of the Article: _____

_____

The 5 W's:

- Who? (Who is the article about?)
- What? (What happened?)
- Where? (Where did it happen?)
- When? (When did it happen?)
- Why? (What are the reasons behind this event?)

Response:

- What do you think about what you read? Personal opinion?
- How does it connect to previous articles you've read on this subject?
- Does this article appear to be biased in any way? How/why?

Level II—News Article Questions

Title of the Newspaper/Magazine: _____

Date of the Newspaper/Magazine: _____

Title and Author/Source of the Article: _____

_____

The 5 Q's:

- In what way might the information in this article affect/influence potential voters?

- In what way does this article address a critical issue/s of this election?
- What does this article contribute to your understanding of the four candidates (presidential and vice presidential)?
- Does the location of the events described (state, city, etc.) in the article have an influence on what happened and/or on how it was reported? If so how? If not, why not?
- Does this article appear to be biased in any way? How/why?

Response:

- What do you think about what you read? Personal opinion?
- How does it connect to previous articles you've read on this subject?
- How might the location of the article in the publication (e.g., opinion page, front page, metro section) influence a reader's response to it?

Figure 6.2. A simple two-tiered homework assignment

Note. Designed with Adrienne Yelsky, Cleveland Heights-University Heights City Schools, and a grant from the Martha Holden Jennings Foundation, 2004.

- All students are doing respectful, valuable work that will allow them to contribute to the larger discussion in the whole classroom community.
- Allowances are made for students to select from a variety of news sources—*The New York Times, Wall Street Journal, Time for Kids*—based on interest and reading level. Teacher and librarian guidance is available to assist here.
- Well-completed assignments are worth the same number of points regardless of the level.

This activity provided a beginning for students and teacher toward a more differentiated classroom. Other activities Ms. Yelsky created later in the semester included a menu of projects that addressed students' learning styles and rubrics that encouraged advanced performance.

Varied Journal Prompts and Book Choices

Other beginning approaches to differentiating instruction might include varied book choices at different levels (for literature circles or book reports) and varied journal prompts. For example:

English/Language Arts

Journal Prompt A (advanced):	How did you feel about Ponyboy's choice to run away with Johnny in *The Outsiders?* What else might he have done?
Journal Prompt 1 (basic):	In this chapter of *The Outsiders*, what did Ponyboy do? Why do you think he made this choice?

Social Studies
(following a discussion of Martin Luther King, Jr.)

Journal Prompt A (basic):	Martin Luther King said "I have a dream . . ." List some of the things you wish for the future of the world.
Journal Prompt 1 (Advanced):	Martin Luther King's "I Have a Dream" speech used a particular oratorical format. Using the same format, write a speech in which you share your hopes for the future of the world.

Next Steps: Increasing Complexity

A somewhat more complex approach can be seen in the following lesson* taught in both a homogeneous advanced class and heterogeneous classes of eighth-grade social studies. Ms. Anderson assessed her students and determined that most knew very little about the Salem Witch Trials. She divided the classes into groups by reading ability and gave each an article or series of articles about the trials at low, medium, or high reading levels. The essential question driving their study was "Why did the Salem Witch Trials occur?" The groups read and discussed their individual articles. In some cases, Ms. Anderson highlighted passages or phrases to help the struggling learners identify the most important ideas. This took a period or two. Following this, she used a jigsaw technique and formed triads of one student from each group to share the key points of their article. This took one class period. The culminating activities were a Socratic seminar and journal entries focused around the original essential question.

What makes this example more complex is the incorporation of multiple instructional and grouping strategies over a longer period of time. Some things to notice about this lesson:

- Even in the supposedly homogeneous advanced class, there was a range of reading abilities. But, more of the students in the advanced class worked with college-level texts.
- A variety of strategies were used that enhanced higher level thinking while ability differences were accommodated.
- Practices were developmentally appropriate: flexible grouping, multiple activities, collaborative seminars.

---

*Lesson designed by Katie Anderson, Cleveland Heights-University Heights City Schools, with a grant from the Martha Holden Jennings Foundation, 2004. Complete plan is in Appendix B.

- The lesson followed an assessment showing that most students lacked knowledge on this topic, which was required by the curriculum and standards.

Tiered Assignments

Both Ms. Yelsky and Ms. Anderson provided examples of "tiered assignments." A tiered assignment is an approach to classroom activities, student assignments, or homework that addresses the challenge of meeting the range of student readiness or ability in any classroom. It is one of the most useful tools for differentiation.

Following content-specific preassessment or identification of other relevant distinguishing learner characteristics, the teacher divides the learning tasks into levels (tiers) from simple to complex, concrete to abstract, knowledge and comprehension to analysis and synthesis, and so forth. He or she then assigns students to complete the activities or assignments at the most appropriate tier. In the first example, Ms. Yelsky used just a tiered homework assignment. In the second example, Ms. Anderson used a multitext approach to tier the activity. In both cases, the teachers continued to expand their repertoire and implementation of differentiation in their classrooms.

The process of fully implementing a differentiated curriculum can seem overwhelming, but these examples demonstrate the possibility of starting small and gradually increasing one's ability to manage multiple activities and assignments. Other, more advanced differentiated activities include learning contracts, learning centers and stations, problem-based learning, and simulations. These are more advanced because they have more groups and individuals doing different activities simultaneously, involve more advance preparation, and require multiple resources for longer periods of time.

Independent and Orbital Studies

Independent studies and springboard or orbital studies are designed to answer the questions "What do I do when I'm done?" or "What should a student do if he or she tests out of a topic or unit of study?" While independent studies can address *any* topic of interest or value to an individual student (following negotiation with the teacher), orbital and springboard studies "orbit around" or "take off from" the specific content being studied. Frequently, these activities complement efforts to compact the curriculum for gifted students.

Combining Strategies

Differentiated instructional strategies complement each other; they're not "either/or." Teachers can used tiered assignments, curriculum compacting, orbital and independent studies, and contracts in the same unit at different times, in different units, or in different components of a class's requirements. For example, a common middle school language arts (or interdisciplinary) class reading is George Orwell's *Animal Farm*. This study includes standard literature outcomes such as identification and understanding of plot, character, setting, theme, symbol, motivation, conflict, figurative language, and irony. Students who, in previous study of short stories or novels, have demonstrated understanding and mastery of these terms and concepts need different activities to extend and expand their ability to read and analyze literature. Therefore, their study guide for the novel might have different questions from the rest of the class, including tiered questions that address diction, tone, mood, point of view, allegory, and fable.

There may also be students who have already read this book who may need an alternate title that addresses the same concepts and skills. Some students may be ready to read both this novel (novella, really, because it is so short) and George Orwell's *1984* and incorporate these with a study of the author. Students with particular interest in politics and government may deepen their understanding through an orbital study of the Russian Revolution and the key figures and events, connecting them to *Animal Farm* in a class presentation that expands the rest of the class's understanding of Orwell's intention. Others who may have interest in language may do orbital studies of propaganda and its role in government and politics. Students with interest in writing may extend their learning to writing a fable about another political event. (These latter activities are orbital studies because they "orbit" around the main concept and content.)

Finally, there are students who complete all their assigned work on this novel in 2 weeks rather than the 4 the teacher had planned. They might then turn to their "Extended Learning" independent study folder, in which they keep their materials on an independent study project of interest to them. This project could be directly related to the subject (such as animal intelligence) or related to some other area of study, such as designing a computer program, preparing for a spelling bee competition, doing practice problems for an upcoming MathCounts competition, working on a Model UN project for social studies class, or reading a novel.

Some students might have an interest in a topic (like archaeology) that is not typically addressed in school and may use this time for research and reading in this area. If all students have an "Extended Learning" folder appropriate to their needs and interests (including those who struggle with learning and may have vocabulary review flashcards, games that review literary terms, or interest-based reading at an appropriate level), then the stigma of having and using this folder may be reduced or eliminated.

Grading and Assessment

How to assess students and assign grades are frequent dilemmas when secondary teachers use differentiation strategies. Luckily, middle schools still have a little more flexibility than high schools, though both are bound by individual districts' report card systems. Most of these need substantial reform to reflect multiple aspects of individual student progress more appropriately and fully.

Whatever grading and reporting system is used, however, at least part of it should reflect individual accomplishment. Even when mastery of grade-level standards and benchmarks are required grade components, student progress reporting also needs to include growth from an individual's starting point.

Teachers should structure grading and assessment procedures and rubrics to provide opportunities for all students to stretch, but also find success. Because student persistence is tied to a balance of hard work and success as a result of that work, competitive grading is a disincentive for this motivation (Tomlinson & Allan, 2000). Digital portfolios, video progress reports, and other modern innovations can help demonstrate and report student achievement in ways that emphasize individual progress. Parent conferences, particularly those in which students participate, can communicate and expand on individual student growth in multiple areas, including achievement of standards, work quality, attitude, work habits, and effort.

These approaches to reporting student progress are consistent with both good middle schools and good gifted education. McEwin, Dickinson, and Jenkins (2003) reiterated the 1995 NMSA position that "assessment and evaluation should emphasize individual progress rather than comparison with other students . . . one effective approach to making student progress reporting more individualized is through the use of student portfolios" (p. 59). Portfolios and other authentic assessment strategies can both document gifted students' mastery of required standards and provide evidence of advanced performance, thus addressing concerns about accountability and challenge.

Assessment and evaluation should not just measure and judge student progress; they should serve as tools to promote learning (Vars, 2003). While many teachers involve students in selecting topics and projects of interest, student involvement in assessment is less common, particularly in this era of externally imposed high-stakes testing. However, engaging students' participation in multiple aspects of this process—including goal setting, establishing evaluation criteria and methods of demonstrating learning, creating rubrics, using peer and self-evaluation, and even reporting performance—enhances the intrinsic motivation necessary to create lifelong learners.

Conclusion

Differentiation of instruction in general education classes with a wide range of students, as well as in gifted and advanced classes, is an important tool in meeting the needs of all students at all levels. It is a significant addition to the structured learning experiences that make up a student's whole day in middle school.

Next Steps . . . Taking Action

There are many fine books on differentiation that can guide interested schools and teachers (see the Additional Resources listed at the end of this chapter). However, there are several basic keys to remember when differentiating for gifted students in middle schools:

1. Differentiation is not a substitute for acceleration or ability-grouped classes (i.e., differentiation in a lower level math class should not stand in for placement in an Algebra class for students with demonstrated readiness).*

*It is here that gifted advocates and some middle school proponents differ. According to McEwin et al. (2003), "heterogeneous assignment of students should be the norm in all middle schools," albeit with the caution that "simply mixing all students together for instruction without carefully articulated instructional strategies does not guarantee improved student learning. Reorganization plans must be comprehensive and accompanied by intensive and continuing professional development if high rates of success are to be achieved" (p. 58).

2. Differentiation is not a substitute for gifted resource room programming because it does not address the social and emotional needs of gifted students, which require a specially trained teacher and a group of intellectual, rather than age, peers.

3. When in-class groupings are used, they should be flexible (varying by interest, ability, learning style, etc.) and short-term since middle school students are particularly sensitive to labeling and its negative social consequences.

4. Mastery of standards should be carefully documented. But, the foundation of differentiation is good concept-based curriculum and important relevant learning.

5. Preassessments should balance significant details of content knowledge and general conceptual understanding, rather than serve as "picky" attempts to uncover all the little things even bright students don't know or remember. The unit posttest can be an excellent tool for preassessment as long as teachers review it for quirky information that may have been part of one instructional sequence, though not typically part of the curriculum. It is not a chance to "catch" kids or show them "they don't know everything," both of which are unfortunate expressions I've heard from middle school classroom teachers.

6. Be sure to inform parents. The grapevine (athletic events, conference nights, etc.) frequently buzzes with discussion of students' projects. When students in the same class are doing different things, parents may be confused, concerned, or angry. An open house early in the school year and a teacher's welcome letter may be appropriate times

to describe how and why you will be differentiating instruction in your classes. While avoiding jargon, you might want to include examples of what differentiation might look like: potentially different homework assignments, varying assessment rubrics, and so forth. At the same time, it is important that parents understand what differentiation does *not* mean and that the diverse academic needs of each student cannot be individually accommodated all the time (Tomlinson & Allan, 2000).

7. Collaborate with your team members. Some middle school students end up creating collages, brochures, charts, PowerPoint presentations—but not a single essay in a whole semester! Our good intentions to use authentic assessment based on a student's visual and artistic learning interests and strengths are laudable, but all students need to refine their writing skills during middle school. Alternatively, all students need some opportunities to demonstrate learning through creative projects, and no student should be limited to just written reports.

8. Thoughtful application of differentiation can provide the opportunity for both choice and challenge, the two essential elements of an appropriate curriculum for gifted students.

9. The best differentiated instruction is designed around significant essential questions and concept-based learning. While curriculum compacting may eliminate repetition of skills instruction, deep and complex learning requires a rich, multifaceted curriculum as its starting point.

10. There are some things that all students need in the same way at the same time. Sometimes, learning experiences are only available to a large group at one time (an arts

event, for example, or high school orientation.) And sometimes a teacher has a dazzling lesson he or she wants all students to experience together as a whole group. These moments should be carefully considered, structured, and implemented in accordance with teachers' understanding of the students and their best professional judgment. Readiness and follow-up activities can then be arranged to be more individually responsive.

11. Blocks of time and their flexible use provide essential opportunities for differentiated instruction. These are also supported by middle school advocates as elements of high-quality middle schools.

References

Erb, T. O. (Ed.). *This we believe . . . and now we must act*. Westerville, OH: National Middle School Association.

Gregory, G. H, & Chapman, C. (2001). *Differentiated instructional strategies: One size doesn't fit all*. Thousand Oaks, CA: Corwin Press.

Heacox, D. (2001). *Differentiating instruction in the regular classroom: How to reach and teach all learners, grades 3–12*. Minneapolis, MN: Free Spirit.

Kingore, B. (2002). *Rubrics and more!* Austin, TX: Professional Associates.

Kingore, B. (2004). *Differentiation: Simplified, realistic, and effective*. Austin, TX: Professional Associates.

Lingren, C. (1970, February). *Individually prescribed instruction*. Paper presentation at the University of Pittsburgh Learning Research and Development Center, Pittsburgh, PA.

McEwin, C. K., Dickinson, T. S., & Jenkins, D. M. (2003). *America's middle schools in the new century: Status and progress*. Westerville, OH: National Middle School Association.

Reis, S. M., Burns, D. E., & Renzulli, J. S. (1992). *Curriculum compacting: The complete guide to modifying the regular curriculum for high-ability students*. Mansfield Center, CT: Creative Learning Press.

Tomlinson, C. A. (2001). *How to differentiate instruction in mixed-ability classrooms.* Alexandria, VA: Association for Supervision and Curriculum Development.

Tomlinson, C. A., & Allan, S. D. (2000). *Leadership for differentiating schools and classrooms.* Alexandria, VA: Association for Supervision and Curriculum Development.

Tomlinson, C. A., & Eidson, C. C. (2003). *Differentiation in practice: Grades 5–9.* Alexandria, VA: Association for Supervision and Curriculum Development.

Vars, G. (2003). Assessment and evaluation that promote learning. In T. O. Erb (Ed.), *This we believe . . . and now we must act* (pp. 78–89). Westerville, OH: National Middle School Association.

Ward, V. (1980). *Differential education for the gifted.* Ventura, CA: Ventura Superintendent of Schools Office.

Winebrenner, S. (2001). *Teaching gifted kids in the regular classroom: Strategies and techniques every teacher can use to meet the academic needs of the gifted and talented* (Rev ed.). Minneapolis, MN: Free Spirit.

Additional Resources

Benjamin, A. (2002). *Differentiated instruction: A guide for middle and high school teachers.* Poughkeepsie, NY: Eye on Education.

Coil, C., & Merritt, D. (2001). *Solving the assessment puzzle piece by piece.* Marion, IL: Pieces of Learning.

Kaplan, S., & Cannon, M. W. (Eds.). (2001). *Lessons from the middle: High-end learning for middle school students.* Waco, TX: Prufrock Press.

McIntosh, J. (Ed.). (1992). *20 ideas for teaching gifted kids in the middle school and high school.* Waco, TX: Prufrock Press.

McIntosh, J. (Ed.). (1994). *20 more ideas for teaching gifted kids in the middle school and high school.* Waco, TX: Prufrock Press.

Northey, S. S. (2005). *Handbook on differentiated instruction for middle and high schools.* Poughkeepsie, NY: Eye on Education.

Tomlinson, C. A. (1999). *The differentiated classroom: Responding to the needs of all learners.* Alexandria, VA: Association for Supervision and Curriculum Development.

Special Populations

Essential Questions

1. What are the unique challenges faced by diverse populations of gifted adolescents?

2. How can middle schools and gifted advocates respond to these challenges in more inclusive ways that support both excellence and equity?

Early adolescence is a time of great change and challenge as children turn into teenagers on their way to young adulthood. Theorists identify five areas of psychosocial development that are of primary significance during adolescence: identity, autonomy, intimacy, sexuality, and achievement. These aspects of development are both psychological and social in nature (Steinberg, 2005). As gifted students resolve these developmental issues, they bring their unique personalities, sensitivities, concerns, and talents to the task. But, for many, their giftedness is not the only way in which they vary from the norms of the dominant middle-class culture.

Subpopulations of gifted students may experience greater difficulties because of their additional differences from the mainstream. These groups include gifted students who have disabilities; those who are gay, lesbian, or bisexual (GLB); those who come from a culture of poverty; and those who are linguistically or culturally diverse (e.g., African American, Hispanic, Native American, English as a second language learners, rural students). Gender is also an important difference, as gifted girls, who should make up 50% of our identified population, seem to face different chal-

> "To be nobody but yourself in a world which is doing its best to make you everybody else means to fight the hardest human battle ever and to never stop fighting."
>
> —e. e. cummings

lenges than those of gifted boys. These other factors may contribute to feelings of difference, isolation, and disconnection from school and academic pursuits that increase in intensity and importance during middle school.

The Three U's

Diverse gifted students frequently are victims of the three U's: underidentification, underrepresentation in programming and service, and underachievement. The results can be long-lasting social and psychological problems, including depression and loneliness, as well as the loss to society of these young people's talents and potential. These special populations need even greater understanding and attention than the typical middle school gifted student.

Underidentification

The first obstacle to serving special populations of gifted students is identifying them. For example, when a student is found to have a learning disability, the IQ score used to determine discrepancy between potential and actual functioning may (if it is high enough) also indicate giftedness. With physical disabilities, assessment tools that are used with typical students may not be appropriate, and there may not be realistic norms for these tests (Willard-Holt, 1999).

Cultural differences and latent prejudices (about both gifted students and minority students) may interfere with an equitable identification process. Language minority students may be overlooked because their language differences may contribute to slower processing times or lower test scores. African American students and those from a culture of generational poverty are also often underidentified because inappropriate or biased tools are used or too much emphasis is placed on teacher recommendation and student behavior. In addition, some studies of African American students suggest that they are increasingly aware of negative stereotypes about their intelligence and are therefore unmotivated when faced with tests of achievement and intelligence (Ford, 2002).

By the time students arrive in middle school, most formal identification has already occurred. But, classroom teachers and counselors need to be aware that they can still consider gifted identification and service during the middle school years, even if students were not identified earlier. Use of multiple criteria, rather than reliance on one specific test, will increase the probability that potentially gifted students will not be missed. Specific outreach to parents of these subpopulations is often necessary to make them aware of identification opportunities and procedures.

Underrepresentation

Even when special populations of gifted students are identified, they are frequently underrepresented in gifted programs and underserved. Some schools have policies or practices that preclude a student from receiving gifted services if he or she is also receiving special-education services. Attention to giftedness could be written into IEPs, but this raises "ownership" questions regarding service and case management. Students in these special populations may not be achieving at grade level in some (or all) subject areas. With the current attention to state standards and formal assessments, schools may neglect enrichment and instead emphasize working with these students on basic skills to get higher test scores and grades in their general education classes. Administrators and teachers may mistakenly see participation in gifted programming as a reward or make it contingent on other classroom performance criteria, rather than more appropriately seeing it as an additional way to meet a student's needs.

Often, it is not just the school that is responsible. Parents may be unaware of paperwork, deadlines, and options for their children, especially as parental involvement in teenagers' school lives decreases in middle and high school. Parents may not perceive the school as a helpful, supportive partner. Again, targeted outreach to parents of historically underserved populations will help increase participation.

Particular subcultures, including the culture of generational poverty that affects people of many races and ethnicities, may also work against students' willing participation in needed services. Counselors, teachers, and mentors can identify when this is occurring and work with students to counteract peer influences and support the sometimes painful transition.

> An individual brings with him/her the hidden rules of the class in which he/she was raised. . . . To move from poverty to middle class . . . an individual must give up relationships for achievement (at least for some period of time) . . . the two things that help one move out of poverty are education and relationships. (Payne, 1996, p. 11)

Underachievement

Underachievement among subgroups of gifted students is one result of being underidentified and underserved. Social and cultural pressures and the emotional isolation many students feel also contribute to underachievement. In middle school, the prevailing negative definition of intellectuals and artists, as well as the social cost of asserting one's giftedness, causes many of our top students in these subpopulations to choose to be "average." The safety and security seem worth the cost. However the loss of potential to the individual, the school, and to society as a whole is staggering. And middle school seems to be the turning point for making many of these choices. If we can identify and appropriately serve these students, they can achieve at high levels and make significant contributions to their schools and their communities.

Others have written more in-depth on each of these topics. This chapter provides an overview of these critical early adolescent issues and is designed to increase sensitivity to the unique needs of each subpopulation. I have provided an extended discussion of issues relating to gifted girls since these students represent half of the population. The references at the end of the chapter will guide readers to explore more deeply the topics and specific subgroups relevant to their particular situations.

Gifted Students With Disabilities

The gifts of students with disabilities (academic, behavioral, or physical) are often hidden by the disability itself, as well as by the school's single-focus attention to it. To address the issue of underidentifying such students, school personnel must overcome the limitations of traditional gifted testing procedures by using the multiple data sources already collected for special-education students, including student products and case study information. The environment in which assessment takes place is especially critical for these students and should differ from that of the general education classroom (Neu, 2003).

The Talent Discovery Assessment Process (TDAP; Baum, Cooper, & Neu, 1996) was designed specifically to identify potential in fifth- through eighth-grade students with disabilities. It uses behavioral observations of students engaged in domain-specific activities. This process, part of the High Hopes project funded by a Javits Act grant, also identifies specific areas in which gifted/disabled students seem to have success: life and physical science, dramatic and visual arts, and engineering.

Following identification, school personnel are encouraged to serve students through a process called "dual differentiation" (Neu, 2003), through which students receive advanced academics and opportunities for talent development (nurturing students' strengths), with accommodations for their behavior limitations (remediating or compensating for the disability). Mentors and other professionals with similar disabilities are essential components of this service, as they provide both content expertise and necessary social-skills training. Additionally, studying eminent people with disabilities seems to increase student persistence and motivation while providing encouragement and support for shaping the behaviors that contribute to success. When differentiated instructional strategies are adjusted to meet the needs of gifted/learning-disabled students, studies have shown improvements in both social and emotional status and academic performance (Baum, Cooper, & Neu, 2001; Baum, Owen, & Dixon, 1991; Olenchak, 1994; Reis, Neu, & McGuire, 1995; Wees, 1993). Positive and encouraging counseling (group or individual) is another essential component in meeting these students' needs. It emphasizes individual strengths and weaknesses, builds coping skills and effective study habits, and assists students through the adolescent transition.

Three areas of disability need special mention because of their relative high frequency: general learning disabilities, gifted students with Attention-Deficit Disorder (ADD) or Attention-Deficit/Hyperactivity Disorder (ADHD), and gifted students with Asperger's Syndrome. Students with these disabilities all share the same problems of underidentification and exclusion from both programs for students with learning problems and programs for the gifted and talented.

The majority of gifted students with disabilities have learning disabilities (Olenchak & Reis, 2002), especially in reading and writing. This population is often "misjudged, misunderstood, and neglected" (p. 177); they are victimized by negative stereotyping, and their positive abilities are often missed by assessment procedures that are primarily verbal. Alternative assessments and projects, as well as means of acquiring knowledge, can mitigate the impact of a learning disability on a student's achievement. The struggle to cope with both high ability and learning problems can create confusion and emotional difficulties for such students and frustration for their teachers.

Often, the gifted behavior is identified before the learning disability because bright students can develop coping and compensation mechanisms that work well through elementary school. But, as the work becomes more challenging in middle school, the disability becomes more problematic. It is often misidentified as defiance or laziness. Negative school experiences reported by gifted college students with learning disabilities included repeated punishment for not turning work in on time, placement in a self-contained special-education class with students who were mentally retarded or developmentally delayed, and poor treatment (such as being called "lazy") by peers and teachers who did not understand discrepancies between their high and low performance or "disorganized" work habits (Olenchak & Reis, 2002, p. 179). The result can be students who have low self-esteem or are unmotivated, disruptive, withdrawn, or oversensitive. Many suffer from emotional problems ranging from anxiety and mild depression to consideration of suicide.

Gifted students with ADD or ADHD first face the problem that their giftedness is initially misdiagnosed as solely an attention-deficit disorder. The essential first step is more careful identification to be sure that a student really has a clinical diagnosis of ADD or hyperactivity, rather than just the restlessness and boredom many gifted students experience in school. Giftedness can mask ADHD, and vice-versa. The higher the IQ, the later the diagnosis of ADHD seems to occur because students are able to "cover" their learning problems with their high intelligence. But, those students with both giftedness and ADHD are at risk for underachievement, as well as social and emotional adjustment problems (Moon, 2002). These students have lower patience and sustained attention than typical children with tasks that are repetitive, unstimulating, or of low interest. But, when presented with high-interest tasks, these students can show sustained attention that is better than typical children. This variance is frustrating for parents and teachers.

Social immaturity (sometimes by as much as 2 or 3 years), which is common in youngsters with ADD or ADHD, is a particular liability during middle school. These adolescents need additional help and support in controlling and expressing emotions and dealing with middle school issues of social inclusion/exclusion. Students also need additional support in organizing materials and time, following directions, and managing distractions. They need individualized attention to their study habits, for example, deciding when having background music is helpful or when they need a barren study carrel to eliminate distractions.

The child with Asperger's Syndrome or Pervasive Developmental Disorder (PDD) often faces the "Rain Man" stereotype of the "idiot-savant" because they frequently have a single area of extraordinary knowledge or expertise. Many people with Asperger's have an above-average IQ and are extremely talented in number skills, math, computer skills, and music; "autistic minds soar in the virtual realms of mathematics, symbols, and code" (Silverman, 2001, p. 181). But, an additional common characteristic of those with PDD or Asperger's is the inability to read, understand social cues, and relate to others. During the exceptionally social middle school years, these students face inner confusion, as well as isolation and exclusion from others.

The gifts and talents of middle school students with disabilities remain untapped resources for meeting their overall needs for

1. success in establishing and feeling comfortable with their *identity*,
2. *autonomy* as learners who can compensate for their disabilities,
3. *intimacy* with mentors and others who are like them in multiple dimensions (ability and disability), and
4. *achievement*.

Appropriate resolution of these adolescent development tasks should prepare gifted students with disabilities for life in high school, as well as later careers and professional pursuits. Attention to both their abilities and their disabilities will contribute to the elimination of underachievement in this special population of gifted students. To ensure this attention, collaboration between special-education teachers and gifted teachers is essential, particularly with regard to educational planning, communication with parents and guardians, and incorporating intellectual challenge with accommodations for the disability. Davis and Rimm (2004) suggested the following to help gifted students with disabilities:

1. Reduce communication limitations through the use of technology or other compensatory devices. Students must be provided with the time and training to become skilled users of these alternative approaches to demonstrate their knowledge, understanding, and creativity at the advanced level of which they are capable.
2. Develop self-concept through social-skills training, establishing high expectations, using appropriate classroom strategies (like peer tutoring and jigsaw groups with other gifted students, self-assessment, and goal setting), providing mentorships with and studies of successful gifted adults with disabilities, encouraging independence, and continuing instruction in high-level, abstract thinking skills.

3. Parent education and involvement to develop understanding of and strategies for dealing with gifted/disabled children.

Gay, Lesbian, and Bisexual (GLB) Gifted Students

Because gender identity and sexuality are key elements of early adolescent growth and development, middle school is a particularly difficult time for teens who are exploring their sexual identity. Being gifted and gay (or even just wondering about sexual orientation) "almost guarantees social, emotional, and intellectual isolation" (Davis & Rimm, 2004, p. 438). Though approximately 4% of adolescents identify themselves as GLB (Steinberg, 2005), many more young people experiment with both homosexuality and heterosexuality before settling on a sexual preference. Because there are so few students openly identified as "doubly different" (gifted and GLB) and very few studies of adolescents who are gifted and gay, many conclusions are drawn from more general studies of GLB teens.

The average coming out age of 21 is part of the normal search for sexual identity, and few gifted gay students admit their sexual orientation until they are in college, partially as a result of students' awareness of society's negative attitudes. Gifted students' increased sensitivities make them more aware of the threatening environment experienced by homosexuals. Insults and physical violence from homophobic peers, teachers, and even family members are prevalent in middle and high school. School may be perceived as an uncomfortable and dangerous place.

As a result of hiding their identity and attempting to "live a lie," GLB students may feel guilty and rejected, and they may suffer low self-esteem to the point of considering suicide. Gay, lesbian, and bisexual students are more likely than all other students to engage in self-destructive behaviors like drug abuse, smoking, risky sex, or running away from home (Davis & Rimm 2004;

Steinberg, 2005). Extreme academic, athletic, or extracurricular accomplishments and overinvolvement may be manifestations of neurotic or compulsive perfectionism rooted in homosexuality. Gifted boys who are gay or bisexual may also be at greater risk for depression and suicide.

> The extreme cruelty, taunting, bullying, and rejection experienced by these boys may make them give up on life. In addition, the confusion of identity that occurs for most adolescents is likely to be overwhelmingly greater for these gifted boys. There is evidence that among eminent men, those who committed suicide are more likely to have been gay or bisexual. (Kerr & Cohn, 2001, p. 145)

In one study, about 30% of all teen suicides were found to be gay and lesbian youth (Cohn, 2003).

The adolescent developmental tasks in the domains of identity, intimacy, and sexuality are challenging for many teenagers, and GLB students face additional difficulties because they are attempting to resolve these issues without the social support and role models readily available to their heterosexual peers. During middle school, these questions are just beginning to arise, and students must be supported while asking and answering them. Name-calling cannot be allowed, and antigay violence and prejudice should be addressed immediately. Because of gifted students' increased sensitivities, lack of adult response to these behaviors is particularly painful and contributes to additional feelings of loneliness, decreased self-esteem, and isolation. Students who are different in both dimensions (ability and sexuality) may attempt to deny one of these significant aspects of their identity.

Educators who deal with gifted students should be aware of the dilemmas faced by GLB adolescents in school and make themselves available to listen, support, and help solve problems so that all students feel safe and accepted. Attitudes of tolerance and inclusiveness need to be encouraged and modeled by school personnel, who must also be aware of how the academic needs and achievement of intellectually gifted youths might interact with underlying issues of sexual orientation.

Gifted Girls

Since the mid 1980s, a great deal of attention has been drawn to gifted girls' school experiences and achievement. Carol Gilligan's 1984 publication *In a Different Voice* proposed a significantly different psychology of women's decision making and morality. The results of her 6-year longitudinal follow-up study of bright girls at a select private school had disturbing implications for gifted girls. In 1992, the American Association for University Women (AAUW) published its report *Shortchanging Girls, Shortchanging America*, which described barriers to the achievement and professional advancement of girls and women. Myra and David Sadker's 1994 book *Failing at Fairness* described the unequal treatment girls receive in our schools, including less-challenging and less-stimulating educational experiences. Mary Pipher's *Reviving Ophelia: Saving the Selves of Adolescent Girls* (1994) popularized the identity struggles of teenage girls and the needs of gifted girls and young women. Sylvia Rimm's study, published as *See Jane Win* (1999) and *How Jane Won* (2001), described the behaviors and attitudes that contributed to the successes of 1,000 women. And, most relevant to this section, Barbara Kerr's (1994) *Smart Girls: A New Psychology of Girls, Women, and Giftedness*, which was originally published in 1985 as *Smart Girls, Gifted Women*, reviews the background literature on the development of gifted women, identifies barriers to their achievement, and suggests options for programming and guidance. What follows is a summary of aspects relevant to gifted girls during their early adolescent middle school years and why they are at risk during this time.

For the first decade of their lives, schools report equal numbers of gifted girls and boys. Throughout elementary school, girls may even do better than boys in verbal intelligence, grade-point averages, and achievement tests. But, from early adolescence (ages 12–14) on, gifted girls have a particularly difficult time, making them

> "The science pipeline is leaking women . . . a leak that begins in middle school ."
>
> —Davis & Rimm, 2004, p. 372

especially vulnerable during middle school (Galbraith & Delisle, 1996; Kerr 1994; Silverman, 2000). Diverse racial and cultural backgrounds only amplify the challenges gifted girls face. In one study, 54% of gifted seventh- and eighth-grade girls chose grade acceleration when it was offered compared to 73% of boys. By 10th grade, more girls have dropped out of gifted programming than boys. Barriers to girls reaching their full potential are both internal and external.

External Barriers

External barriers are those influences, whether perceived or real, that come from families, institutions, peer groups, the media, or others surrounding an individual.

As gifted girls enter adolescence and explore their identities, they become particularly sensitive to conflicting societal views of women's roles and responsibilities. Evidence of this conflict is reflected in underachievement (particularly in math and science), loss of confidence and self-esteem, decreased standardized test scores (compared to male counterparts), decreased social status and popularity, decreased IQ, low achievement motivation, insecurity, and social isolation. Some researchers have found that, when compared to boys with high grade-point averages, girls with similar grades are more depressed and have more psychosomatic symptoms and lower self-esteem. For high-achieving middle school boys, their self-image scores increase as their grades increase. But, for girls, it is just the opposite. The extent to which any individual girl experiences these is dependent upon how willing she is to expose her full abilities and intellect to her peers and the amount of support she receives at home and at school.

Socialization processes result in gifted girls losing their self-confidence and lowering their aspirations. For example, cultural do's and don'ts imposed on girls in middle school make it hard for them to display their intelligence and pursue excellence as aggressively as boys. Girls are expected by society to be "good," "pretty," and "well-adjusted." Society encourages boys to show superior intellectual ability to attract members of the opposite sex, while girls' self-confidence is lost when even bright males consider their attractiveness more important than their intelligence.

Davis and Rimm (2004) studied gifted girls with high math aptitude and found that many of them are not placed in (or choose not to enroll in) high-level math. Girls may see success in math as contradictory to peers' expectations of their roles, and they may believe that boys do not like girls who excel in math. Therefore, they may choose not to develop their mathematical abilities. Their lack of advanced knowledge and skill in math and science have long-lasting effects on later test scores, high school course selections, and career and college opportunities. Girls' computer use also declines in adolescence.

As adolescent girls work at establishing their identity as women, additional confusion may result as they try to understand how their sexuality (conception, childbirth, etc.) fits with achievement in demanding fields. They fear having to choose between career and marriage. Modern women receive conflicting messages about "accomplishment versus caretaking" and are held back by their own "fear of success" (Streznewski, 1999, p. 213).

While bright students are told to develop their talents and be selfishly single-minded in pursuit of their goals, women are simultaneously expected to be selfless, nurturing, and supportive of others. Societal expectations of docility and conformity lead to underachievement for gifted girls as they decrease the risk-taking behaviors of asking provocative questions, challenging authority, or guessing at answers. The pressures of society limits a girls' aspirations beginning in early adolescence as she is encouraged to adjust, adapt, and possibly abandon her dreams (Kerr, 1994).

School materials (texts, films), books, toys and games, as well as the popular media (movies, TV, magazines) portray gender stereotypes and lack inclusion of women's accomplishments. Girls see predominantly male examples of leaders, politicians, artists, musicians, and inventors and too few gifted female role models.

Home influences are the most significant influence on academic achievement and perceptions, and parental expectation can either carry on or challenge the larger culture's stereotypes. Negative messages sent by parents can include admonitions to act ladylike, be quiet, be subservient, be helpful, don't speak out, or dress a certain way (which often restricts kinds of participation). Fathers seem to have a particularly influential role during adolescence. They often overly praise their daughters for their appearance, fashion sense, or popularity. Both parents may overemphasize the value of a busy social life, often causing girls to make excessive compromises to be popular and please others. Some parents become concerned that their daughters will not be happy, accepted, and likeable if they are too different. They switch their positive reinforcement and comments to appearance and social life, paying less attention to academic and intellectual achievement. But, parents who openly appreciate and encourage their daughter's talents and abilities throughout adolescence and especially during the critical early years contribute positively to lasting self-image and accomplishments.

Teacher expectations, either overt or subtle, may unconsciously discourage females from developing their talent equally with males. Boys receive more attention from teachers than girls in classrooms and receive more specific and informative feedback, including both praise and criticism (Kloosterman & Suranna, 2003). Terms like "bossy" and "overachiever," commonly applied to capable and assertive girls, should be eliminated (Silverman, 2000). The former denigrates girls' leadership talents, and the latter implies that she is using hard work to make up for lack of ability. Both deny gifted girls' exceptional talents and achievement potential.

Because girls are more successful at hiding intelligence and silencing their voices, teachers are usually less able to identify those who are gifted. Male teachers seem to identify and perceive gifted girls differently from female teachers who, especially in math and science, can have a positive and encouraging effect and can serve as role models. Counselors too can help by supporting women's high achievement and encouraging adolescent girls to participate in appropriate high-level classes and other accelerated opportunities.

Internal Barriers

Three internal factors contribute to underachievement in gifted adolescent girls: low sense of competence, attributional differences (i.e., what attributes lead to success), and low achievement motivation.

Gifted girls begin to lose self-confidence and belief in their abilities late in elementary school, a decline that continues through college and graduate school. The "fear of success" syndrome holds young gifted women back because they believe that success and achievement will lead to rejection by their peers and families. Additionally, girls avoid competition in order to preserve relationships with both boys and other girls.

Multipotentiality, rather than being perceived as an asset, is often a confusing liability. Gifted girls enter middle school being told "you can do anything you want." For some, having so many choices opens options; for others, it means they are unable to find their own niche or choose a single vocational or academic path since it is not possible to do everything they would like to do and are capable of doing.

Perfectionism occurs when girls internalize unrealistic "Superwoman/Supergirl" expectations. They set unreasonable goals for themselves, creating impossible pressure. Gifted girls seem to experience excessive anxiety and concern over mistakes, often based on perceived or real parental expectations and criticisms. They strive not just to be capable, but perfect—in their own eyes, as well as others'. Girls get rewarded for their sensitivity to what others want and need. They are so eager to please others and be what others want them to be that they learn to be content using only a small part of their potential.

Eating disorders (e.g., anorexia nervosa and bulimia nervosa) seem to be overrepresented in competitive educational settings, particularly among girls and those in the upper classes (Garner, 1991). They are related to the struggle to live up to excessive achievement standards and may also be connected to some young women's role conflicts. Eating disorders may also be connected to the asynchronous development of some adolescent gifted girls (Garner).

The attributional differences between gifted adolescent boys and girls have a significant impact on their attitudes and behaviors. Girls tend to attribute their success to hard work or luck and their failures or struggles to lack of ability, while males do the opposite. Girls think they have to work harder than boys, who are perceived as "just smarter." Too many gifted adolescent girls believe that high ability means they should be able to achieve good grades without work, a misperception that is based at least in part on "sliding by" in elementary school. Facing challenges in middle school can potentially cause a drop in confidence unless girls learn to accept and persist in challenging tasks. Appropriate attribution can be taught through all-girl group guidance experiences, encouragement of leadership, assertiveness training, bibliotherapy, mentorships and internships, and other opportunities that directly deal with issues of femininity, self-confidence, and achievement orientation.

Low achievement motivation in girls occurs in part because achievement and affiliation are perceived as opposites. Middle school gifted girls may avoid displays of outstanding intellectual ability and search for better ways to conform to the norm of the peer group. Gifted girls can face torment from both boys and girls if they choose achievement over conformity. They fear social isolation as a consequence of success, so girls "play dumb" fearing that "smart" equals "less attractive and less socially competent." In their early teens, gifted girls often sacrifice their gifted friends to gain the acceptance of less-capable classmates; they deny, camouflage, or abandon their talents and will not leave their friends for the opportunity of acceleration. They worry about the impact of their giftedness on others (Silverman, 2000)

Overcoming Barriers

Girls must receive guidance in examining and confronting women's underrepresentation in nontraditional careers, inequities in salaries, and the lack of affordable childcare when trying to balance family and professional life. The pursuit of popularity should be deemphasized for gifted girls. It is clear that gifted girls need mentors and successful female role models, as well as high-achieving girlfriends who share advanced school experiences and similar interests. They can help each other deal with teasing from boys and negative attitudes that seem to peak in ninth grade (Silverman, 2000) as they support each other's love of learning and passionate intellectual interests.

Even those who are highly motivated to achieve must overcome society's message that the worlds of high-power careers and femininity are mutually exclusive. Identity, autonomy, intimacy, sexuality, and achievement are all connected for gifted girls, and societies and cultures can change their attitudes and behaviors in order to create a more hospitable environment for their growth and development.

Culturally, Linguistically, Economically, and Ethnically Diverse Gifted Students

Gifted adolescents who are members of cultural, linguistic, and ethnic minorities, as well as those from low-economic back-

WOW: Women on Wednesdays

Alexis, Holly, and Megan, three gifted eighth graders, asked to speak to me.

"We need a women's group," they said, and they went on to describe what they envisioned: a chance for middle school girls to get together and address problems unique to being female in our school. Seeing this as an opportunity to address their concerns *and* build leadership, I worked with them to create an announcement inviting all interested girls to an organizational meeting in the guidance counselor's office.

We were surprised when more than a third of the girls in the school showed up! Clearly, there was a need here.

The group called itself "WOW: Women on Wednesdays," named after our meeting day. Over the course of the school year, the girls planned a series of meetings and events, and they rotated roles as facilitator, materials manager, and publicity coordinator. Discussion topics ranged from "my favorite piece of clothing" to "overcoming resistance to speaking out in class." During Women's History month, the students organized a whole-school assembly about gender differences. We made and shared "Identity Bag Collages" to show who we were outside and who we were inside. Various speakers addressed the group, including a local female OB/GYN who specialized in adolescents. The girls created a pamphlet of drawings and poems that addressed these issues, some of which they created themselves and some of which were written by significant women writers.

None of us has ever forgotten the excitement, power, and value of this group—finding a strong voice, sharing concerns, and exploring together our identities as women.

grounds, face their own sets of unique barriers and challenges. They, like students with disabilities, are underidentified and underrepresented in gifted programs. In many cases, the values and behaviors of the teen subcultures work against their developing a "scholar identity" (D. Y. Ford, personal communication, 2005), and schools rarely offer adequate and comprehensive antidotes to these pressures for underachievement. Without intervention, minority students and those from poverty may turn away from school and mainstream society and use their talents for negative and potentially destructive purposes (Kelble, 2003). In order to ensure equity and encourage excellence, gifted advocates must take steps to identify, involve, and support gifted students who are culturally, linguistically, and ethnically diverse (CLED).

During early adolescence, when young men and women are attempting to explore and create their identities, figuring out how to keep their cultural roots while reaching out into the world of academics and intellectual pursuits is a demanding and daunting task. When poverty and economic disadvantage are factored in, the obstacles to gifted and talented minority students reaching their full potential may seem overwhelming. Cultural difference is too often perceived by school personnel as a cultural deficit (Tomlinson, Ford, Reis, Briggs, & Strickland, 2004), and incongruity between home culture and school culture create internal conflicts. Students experience battles of loyalty between the dominant cultural value of individual achievement and their heritage, traditions, and community.

The culture of poverty tends to limit expectations and possibilities for all cultural and ethnic groups, although there is a greater likelihood of Black and Hispanic children being poor than White children (Payne, 1996). Poor and minority children's differences from middle-class values and practices in cognitive processing, language use, and general knowledge are perceived as a deficit, and this perception hinders students' academic and intellectual progress (Ford & Harmon, 2001; Payne).

Gifted adolescents from economically disadvantaged environments are vulnerable to negative influences in their neighborhoods. When their talents are not recognized and positively channeled, their high abilities make them excellent potential leaders in destructive social groups and behaviors.

The largest population of culturally diverse students in the total school population of the United States are African Americans (Tomlinson et al., 2004). Values in the African-American community tend to be more "communal, emotional, person-centered, and flexible" than the dominant culture (Tomlinson et al., p. 27). Being female compounds the challenges for gifted Black girls. They are at greater risk for underachievement, dropping out, and school failure than are White females (Ford, 1996). While Asian American students sometimes face intense pressures to excel, African American teens are sometimes criticized and accused of "acting White" when they are high achievers. Gifted Asian American and Hispanic girls may face resistance to demonstrating their abilities and talents from strongly patriarchal families with clearly delineated gender roles (Kloosterman & Suranna, 2003).

Native American gifted students may be the least understood because of the huge diversity in tribal languages, customs, history, concerns, and values. Hispanic and Asian American students are also often misperceived as homogeneous despite great differences in country of origin, social class, family structure and dynamics, and culture. But, there are some common themes that seem to connect many of these diverse groups: focus on community, rather than an individual's accomplishments; strong connection to religion and home location; emphasis on cooperation and harmony, rather than competitiveness; and emphasis on oral, rather than written expression. Language barriers, as well as cultural values that emphasize deference and self-effacement, may cause some CLED students to limit oral class participation, which might draw attention to their individual abilities and achievements. Clear male-female role divisions may create dilemmas in achievement motivation for girls, as well as problems for "feminine" boys who have artistic and creative talents.

Portfolio and alternative assessments (e.g., the Naglieri Nonverbal Ability Test) may be more effective in increasing identification and overcoming the limitations of traditional written and timed tests. Culturally responsive teaching methods must be incorporated into gifted programs and classes to create inviting environments that draw on and value CLED gifted students' cultural knowledge, prior experiences, and learning styles. With disadvantaged students, sincere and caring teachers are critical, acting as both mentors and empathetic adult listeners.

Assistance in accessing available resources and opportunities can help students find a balance among a positive racial and ethnic identity and academic and intellectual achievements. Helping students understand their own learning styles and developing appropriate complementary educational experiences can also increase students' academic participation and school success. These must both address gaps in skill development and include challenging curricula that reflect students' interests and perceptions. Students also need training in conflict resolution and leadership development to help them learn nonviolent ways to resolve problems and address injustices.

The multiculturalism that has become more prevalent in traditional curricula must also be reflected in the content and materials of gifted programs, but not just as add-ons or during holidays. Rather, the whole curriculum must be structured to empower students to understand multiple perspectives on issues and events and encourage them to take action to help solve important social issues (Ford & Harmon, 2001). Culturally diverse people and viewpoints, both in literature and as mentors and role models, must be included in students' experiences. The issue of differentiation that is so much a part of gifted education must extend to matching appropriate teaching and learning to CLED gifted learners. For students of poverty, for example, it includes building an additional and different set of cognitive and

Gifted Students Need . . .	Culturally Diverse Students Need . . .
higher level thinking skills	relevant and real-world experiences
acceleration	identity enhancement
enrichment	culturally compatible teaching styles
in-depth study	tactile and kinesthetic learning
attention to social/affective needs and development	social and cooperative learning

Figure 7.1. Gifted and culturally diverse student needs

linguistic processes through graphic organizers and visual relationships and support systems and direct teaching of the hidden middle-class rules that permeate schools (Payne, 1996). It also includes making content, process, and product modifications that are simultaneously responsive to both sets of student needs (Tomlinson et al., 2004).

Building relationships is critical. While advocating for the students, we must not just accept, but welcome participation of parents and families. We must help them to understand their children's gifts and talents and to connect with schools and programs. When appropriate, parent communications and contacts may be provided in the families' home language. Through these contacts, we can become more effective teachers as we learn more about our students and their cultures. By providing emotional support to students and families, we can allow students to take risks. We can also demonstrate that we value and respect these cultures. From within these cultures we can find tutors and mentors for our students. With adolescents, we can use this knowledge to help them

Hip-Hop Advisory: Reaching Out

As the gifted teacher at our middle school, I didn't feel I had enough contact with the increasing population of African American students. Many had transferred to our district after most gifted identification had taken place, and although some Black students were in the gifted program, I suspected that there should be more.

Our Blue Ribbon School's advisory program had two components: the core group that stayed together all school year and met 3 days a week and interest advisories that changed every quarter and met 2 days a week. My colleague Jill Goodman and I decided to offer a hip-hop advisory to connect with the interests of many of our Black students. Parents had to sign permission slips allowing their children to participate because of the potential for inappropriate language or provocative discussion topics (although the students were careful almost to a fault to ensure that only "school-appropriate" versions of songs were brought to class). Students who rarely remembered homework or other administrative paperwork had these forms in the next day!

The group was made up of about 20 African American students and 2 White students. In collaboration with the Cleveland-based Rock and Roll Hall of Fame, we studied the history and culture of hip-hop, discussed the relationships described in various songs, and listened to the music of popular groups. The students taught us (almost!) how to freestyle, and we taught them (almost!) appreciation for diverse opinions and how to express and accept them.

The ripple effect on raising teachers' expectations for these students was immediate—though it revealed prejudices none of us felt comfortable admitting. Strong relationships were built between the students and the two of us that lasted years after the group was over. Hopefully, students saw "the gifted teacher" in a different light. When the quarter ended, students pleaded to continue the group, but as a school we had decided that these interest groups should be exploratory in nature and students should rotate through four choices over the course of the year. In retrospect, it might have been better to keep us all together.

The lessons I learned have been lasting, and I hope they were for the students, as well. School activities like this can build common ground where diverse cultures are valued and students' interests are considered in programming in both gifted and general education classes.

through issues of identity formation, increasing autonomy, and achieving their potential.

For example, Project GEAR UP (Gaining Early Awareness and Readiness for Undergraduate Programs) starts at the sixth and seventh grades and continues through high school. Using partnerships, it provides information to students and parents about post-high school opportunities and financial aid. It recognizes the importance of early intervention to help students discover and develop their abilities and to connect them with resources about all aspects of college life and career options.

Conclusion

The team structure of the middle school and the philosophical emphasis on meeting the needs of individual adolescents lend themselves to providing the extra attention and support that subpopulations of gifted students need during this transitional period. Counselors and teachers can work with students and parents to increase achievement, motivation, and development of Ford's "scholar identity." Sensitivity to cultural connections will allow students to feel that they can belong in multiple settings without having to sacrifice a piece of themselves. Making appropriate accommodations for gifted students with special needs will redefine the concept of "least-restrictive alternative."

Gifted education has failed many students from diverse backgrounds (Tomlinson et al., 2004), and it is imperative that we reverse this failure. We must seize the turning point of middle school to turn students toward making the most of their talents and abilities and help them integrate all aspects of their selves: psychological, cultural, physical, academic and intellectual, social, and sexual. It is never too late to help students discover their gifts and turn their lives toward success and wholeness.

Next Steps . . . Taking Action

1. Analyze all curricular materials and identification instruments, policies, and procedures for racism and sexism. Ensure that appropriate identification instruments are used that can help find "invisible" populations of gifted students, particularly those that might have been overlooked during elementary school because of disabilities or cultural and gender stereotypes.

2. Use teaching methods that are sensitive and responsive to students of varying cultures and genders and those with different learning styles and disabilities.

3. Use appropriate guidance, counseling, and support techniques to reach out to diverse gifted students and their families.

4. All school personnel should work to ensure that their language is free of bias. They should also help increase

students' awareness of the language they use and the effect certain words have on others.

5. A wide variety of mentors and role models should be connected with individuals and groups of students, matching gifted students' backgrounds, gender, and needs with the backgrounds, gender, and strengths of the adults.

6. As much as possible, teachers should be knowledgeable about and sensitive to the cultures, ethnic groups, and linguistic diversity in their schools and their attitudes toward giftedness and talent.

7. Students in special populations should be helped to understand their own unique potential, talents, and abilities. They should be encouraged to participate in challenging courses and enrichment programs and provided with the support that allows them to withstand and understand the range of potential social and cultural responses to their choices.

References

American Association for University Women. (1992). *Shortchanging girls, shortchanging America*. Washington, DC: Author.

Baum, S., Cooper, C. R., & Neu, T. W. (1996, Spring). Project High Hopes: Identifying and nurturing talent in students with special needs. *TAG Update*, 7–8.

Baum, S. M., Cooper, C. R., & Neu, T. W. (2001). Dual differentiation: An approach for meeting the curricular needs of gifted students with learning disabilities. *Psychology in the Schools, 38*, 156–165.

Baum, S., Owen, S. V., & Dixon, J. (1991). *To be gifted and learning disabled: From definitions to practical intervention strategies*. Mansfield Center, CT: Creative Learning Press.

Cohn, S. (2003). The gay gifted learner: Facing the challenge of homophobia and anti-homosexual bias in schools. In J. A. Castellano (Ed.), *Special populations in gifted education: Working with diverse gifted learners* (pp. 123–134). Boston: Allyn and Bacon.

Davis, G. A., & Rimm, S. B. (2004). *Education of the gifted and talented* (5th ed.). Boston: Pearson Education.

Ford, D. Y. (1996). *Reversing underachievement among gifted Black students: Promising practices and programs.* New York: Teachers College Press.

Ford, D. Y. (2002). Racial identity among gifted African American students. In M. Neihart, S. M. Reis, N. M. Robinson, & S. M. Moon (Eds.), *The social and emotional development of gifted children: What do we know?* (pp. 155–164). Waco, TX: Prufrock Press.

Ford, D. Y., & Harmon, D. (2001). Equity and excellence: Providing access to gifted education for culturally diverse students. *Journal of Secondary Gifted Education, 12,* 141–147.

Galbraith, J., & Delisle, J. (1996). *The gifted kids' survival guide: A teen handbook.* Minneapolis, MN: Free Spirit.

Garner, D. M. (1991). Eating disorders in the gifted adolescent. In M. Bireley & J. Genshaft (Eds.), *Understanding the gifted adolescent: Educational, developmental, and multicultural issues* (pp. 50–64). New York: Teachers College Press.

Gilligan, C. (1984). *In a different voice: Psychology theory and women's development.* Cambridge, MA: Harvard University Press.

Kelble, E. (2003). Reflections on special programming for the gifted disadvantaged student. In J. F. Smutny (Ed.), *Designing and developing programs for gifted students* (pp. 86–94). Thousand Oaks, CA: Corwin Press.

Kerr, B. (1985). *Smart girls, gifted women.* Columbus: Ohio Psychology Press.

Kerr, B. (1994). *Smart girls: A new psychology of girls, women, and giftedness* (Rev. ed.). Scottsdale, AZ: Great Potential Press.

Kerr, B. A., & Cohn, S. J. (2001). *Smart boys: Talent, manhood, and the search for meaning.* Scottsdale, AZ: Great Potential Press.

Kloosterman, V., & Suranna, K. (2003). Gifted and talented females: The struggle for recognition. In J. A. Castellano (Ed.), *Special populations in gifted education: Working with diverse gifted learners* (pp. 97–111). Boston: Allyn and Bacon.

Moon, S. M. (2002). Gifted children with Attention-Deficit/ Hyperactivity Disorder. In M. Neihart, S. M. Reis, N. M. Robinson, & S. M. Moon (Eds.), *The social and emotional development of gifted children: What do we know?* (pp. 193–201). Waco, TX: Prufrock Press.

Neu, T. (2003). When the gifts are camouflaged by disability. In J. A. Castellano (Ed.), *Special populations in gifted education: Working with diverse gifted learners* (pp. 151–162). Boston: Allyn and Bacon.

Olenchak, F. R. (1994). Talent development: Accommodating the social and emotional needs of secondary gifted/learning disabled students. *Journal of Secondary Gifted Education, 5*(3), 40–52.

Olenchak, F. R., & Reis, S. M. (2002). Gifted students with learning disabilities. In M. Neihart, S. M. Reis, N. M. Robinson, & S. M. Moon (Eds.), *The social and emotional development of gifted children: What do we know?* (pp. 177–191). Waco, TX: Prufrock Press.

Payne, R. K. (1996). *A framework for understanding poverty.* Highlander, TX: aha! Process.

Pipher, M. (1994). *Reviving Ophelia: Saving the selves of adolescent girls.* New York: Ballantine Books.

Reis, S. M., Neu, T. W., & McGuire, J. (1995). *Talent in two places: Case students of high ability students with learning disabilities who have achieved* (Research Monograph No. 95114). Storrs: National Research Center on the Gifted and Talented, University of Connecticut.

Rimm, S. B. (1999). *See Jane win: The Rimm report on how 1,000 girls became successful women.* New York: Crown.

Rimm, S. B. (2001). *How Jane won: 55 successful women share how they grew from ordinary girls to extraordinary women.* New York: Crown.

Sadker, M., & Sadker, D. (1994). *Failing at fairness: How America's schools cheat girls.* New York: Scribner.

Silverman, L. K. (Ed.). (2000). *Counseling the gifted and talented.* Denver, CO: Love.

Silverman, S. (2001, December). The geek syndrome. *Wired,* 175–183

Steinberg, L. (2005). *Adolescence* (7th ed.). New York: McGraw Hill.

Streznewski, M. K. (1999). *Gifted grownups: The mixed blessings of extraordinary potential.* New York: Wiley.

Tomlinson, C. A., Ford, D. Y., Reis, S. M., Briggs, C. J., & Strickland, C. A. (2004). *In search of the dream: Designing schools and classrooms that work for high potential students from diverse cultural backgrounds.* Washington, DC: National Association for Gifted Children.

Wees, J. (1993). Gifted/learning disabled: Yes, they exist and here are some successful ways to teach them. *Gifted International, 8*(1), 48–51.

Willard-Holt, C. (1999). *Dual exceptionalities* (ERIC Digest #E574). Reston, VA: ERIC Clearinghouse on Disabilities and Gifted Education.

Additional Resources

Baldwin, A. Y. (Ed.). (2004). *Culturally diverse and underserved populations of gifted students.* Thousand Oaks, CA: Corwin Press.

Boothe, D., & Stanley, J. C. (2004). *In the eyes of the beholder: Critical issues for diversity in gifted education.* Waco, TX: Prufrock Press.

Castellano, J. A. (Ed.). (2003). *Special populations in gifted education: Working with diverse gifted learners.* Boston: Allyn and Bacon.

Delisle, J., & Galbraith, J. (2002). *When gifted kids don't have all the answers: How to meet their social and emotional needs.* Minneapolis, MN: Free Spirit.

Estes, C. P. (1992). *Women who run with the wolves.* New York: Ballantine Books.

Ford, D. Y. (1996). *Reversing underachievement among gifted Black students: Promising practices and programs.* New York: Teachers College Press.

Neihart, M., Reis, S. M., Robinson, N. M., & Moon, S. M. (Eds.). (2002). *The social and emotional development of gifted children: What do we know?* Waco, TX: Prufrock Press.

Books, Reading, and Gifted Middle School Students

Essential Questions

1. How can books and reading instruction be used as essential elements of middle school gifted programming?

2. In what ways might engagement with books help gifted students' cognitive and social/emotional growth?

3. What reading materials and book titles would be particularly valuable for middle school gifted students?

Why a whole separate chapter on books and reading? Why not one on math? Or science? History? Or technology? Because reading is the key to learning in any subject area. Thompson (2001) called the language arts "the core of all content," reminding us that "students who function at high levels in language arts gain a strength that becomes strong in all subjects."

Middle school is the time when we lose many students to other time-consuming pursuits: computer games, the Internet, instant messaging, socializing, clubs, arts lessons, and sports. Young teens may lose their commitment to books as an important part of their recreational and intellectual lives. As with any other activity, the less time devoted to reading, the less adept one becomes. Without continuing to read at increasingly advanced levels, students' comprehension skills, as well as those in vocabu-

lary and syntax (essential tools of sophisticated writers, the partner of good readers), remain stagnant.

Tomlinson (1992) pointed out middle schools' consistent tendency to "teach to the middle," and Vacca, Vacca, and Grove
(1991) agreed that teachers sometimes hold gifted students back.
Many English/language arts programs, even in middle schools,
continue to be anchored to a basal reader and focused on basic
skills instruction to increase reading achievement scores (Reis,
2001). Instead, "Abilities and interests should control the reading
curriculum" for gifted students (Baskin, 1998, p. 68).

Planning Instruction

Equity requires that the needs and exceptionality of gifted
readers be recognized and that appropriate educational programming be provided. Slavin (1999) has advocated dividing middle
school students into three groups according to reading skills: at or
above grade level, below grade level, and barely reading. But this
still fails to address fully the needs of the gifted reader. Jackson
and Davis' (2000) suggestion that "more advanced learners also
might spend some of their reading acceleration time learning a
foreign language, tutoring younger students or engaged in other
activities connected to the curriculum" (p. 91) also misses the
point. Baskin (1998, p. 68) suggested implementing the following
responsive practices to meet the reading needs of gifted students:

1. design beneficial settings;
2. select suitable and challenging reading material;
3. deemphasize grades and focus more on process than
    product;
4. reassess the implications of accountability with its stress
    on minimum standards; and
5. enrich instruction to reverse the underachievement of
    some gifted students.

In schools, we can blend direct classroom instruction and open discussion. We can combine content-based study (historical facts and concepts when reading historical fiction, literary analysis when reading novels, etc.) with counseling conversations around issues of identity, acceptance, understanding of feelings, goal setting, and conflict resolution. Throughout, we can stress the important critical thinking skills of analysis, drawing conclusions, inferencing, solving problems, and making judgments that ultimately inform students' attitudes and behavior. Books can help gifted adolescents cope with the problems they face as unique individuals in an often unappreciative and unwelcoming school and societal environment.

Sessions or classes where the focus is on connecting gifted students' developmental needs with characters and issues in a text should follow a sequence similar to the following:

1. Warm-up or introductory activity to generate interest and focus on the essential questions.
2. Student reading of and reflection on the text (in sections or as a whole.) Students may read totally independently or may be guided by reader response journals, reflection questions, study guides, or other teacher-designed materials.
3. Book discussion that revolves around student questions, concerns, connections, feelings, interpretation, and understanding, rather than specific plot or reading comprehension questions.
4. Culminating product that demonstrates student understanding or response.

Bibliotherapy

For any adolescent who feels different, books can be both comfort and company. Through reading, gifted students can meet others who are like them and who are facing or have triumphed over the same dilemmas they face (Delisle & Galbraith, 2002; Schroeder-Davis, 1992). Novels and their characters provide opportunities to explore

> "We read to discover we are not alone."
>
> —C. S. Lewis in the film *Shadowlands* (1993)

identities and actions in a safe fictional environment. Fantasy and science fiction novels, favorites among gifted students, offer stress-relieving escape and relaxation, as well as insight and sometimes humor. Biographies and autobiographies provide glimpses into the lives of talented, successful men and women and how they overcame obstacles to their achievements, whether internal, societal, cultural, or familial.

Books offer a bridge to students' deeper feelings and questions. In homogeneous gifted language arts or reading classes or gifted pull-out groups, as well as in targeted book clubs and library book discussion groups, reading and sharing responses to relevant and interesting books can play a key role in students' intellectual and emotional growth.

Bibliotherapy is the use of literature to "bring about a therapeutic interaction between participant and facilitator" (Hynes & Hynes-Berry, 1987, pp. 9–10). While clinical bibliotherapy is for individuals with behavioral or emotional problems and requires skilled psychotherapeutic professionals, developmental bibliotherapy can be facilitated by teachers, counselors, librarians, or other school personnel, as well as by parents. It can address students' needs as they progress through normal stages of growth and self-understanding. As such, it is a powerful tool for responding to the affective needs of gifted students and their questioning and concerns as they try to understand themselves and their experiences (Hébert & Kent, 2000). In order for bibliotherapy to be effective, the reader must identify with the character(s) in the book, share an emotional connection to the character(s), and gain insights by relating the experiences in the book to his or her own life (Halsted, 2002). This process needs to be facilitated by the teacher or leader.

Bibliotherapy can be an aid to personal problem solving and social adaptation (Reynales, 1978), and it can address issues such as exceptionally high expectations (by self and others), self-criticism and perfectionism, conformity and rejection, dealing with stress and pressure, and demands of the artist's life. Gifted students' intellectual and emotional intensity may place them at additional risk for depression and self-destructive behavior, and bibliotherapy sessions can help alert us to students who may be in trouble (Kerr, 1991; Silverman, 2000).

Subpopulations, such as culturally diverse gifted students or gifted boys, may also benefit from bibliotherapy.

> Guided reading requires a meaningful follow-up discussion. To simply read a good biography . . . is not bibliotherapy. It is very important that [students] become involved in discussions, counseling, and follow-up techniques such as role-playing and creative problem solving. . . . A bibliotherapy program through biography (and other literature) can become the basis of solid introspection for gifted students when presented in this manner. From the self-knowledge gained from the experience, the trust for meaningful relationships may develop. In addition, the discussion follow-ups provide points of adult modeling and interpersonal contact that may be invaluable. (Hébert, 1995, p. 211)

Selecting Materials

Precocious reading ability can create a dilemma for many early adolescents and their parents and teachers. Many gifted students are voracious readers, especially through elementary school. By middle school, most are able to read high school and college texts and adult materials. But, this is coupled with age-appropriate teen concerns. Just because a student can read adult materials doesn't mean he or she should or even wants to.

The pairing of specific teens with the right books at the right times requires understanding of each individual student, as well as knowledge of the available literature. The Reading Interest-A-Lyzer (Renzulli, 1997; see Reis, Gubbins, & Richards, 2002, pp. 42–44) is a tool to help teachers match students with books. "When talented readers have the opportunity to read high-quality, high-interest books as a result of curriculum modification techniques, there is a greater likelihood that the combination of interest and flexibility may lead to a learning explosion" (Richards, 2001, p. 4).

Many gifted adolescents want (and need) to read books about sports, dating, friendships, parents, problems (e.g., suicide, drugs, anorexia), cultural identity, sexuality, and school. They especially enjoy books with a good sense of humor and a sarcastic or satiric look at the world. The popularity of Douglas Adams' *The Hitchhiker's Guide to the Galaxy* (1980) among gifted students—especially boys—is testimony to this.

Over the years, young adult literature has moved from being primarily for less-motivated and less-able students to an increasingly rich source of books to meet the abilities of all readers. There are many well-written young adult novels that provide gifted students with material for both introspection and literary analysis. But, gifted and typical teen readers differ significantly in the levels of thinking and analysis they are prepared to bring to a text, their expectations of literary quality and complexity, their ability to sustain effort with longer books, and the intensity with which they experience the characters' and their own feelings.

Young adult books can also provide a bridge to more classic literature. Some excellent suggestions for creating this bridge can be found in *From Hinton to Hamlet* (Herz & Gallo, 1996), which provides specific titles from young adult and classic literature connected by theme, such as pairing *Downriver* by Will Hobbs with *Lord of the Flies* by William Golding. Both deal with leaders' abuses of power and loss of innocence.

Classics, in part because they are by established gifted writers and often have gifted characters and in part because of their time-tested universal themes, may also provide opportunities for meaningful conversations. "The fact that one never really gets to the bottom of a great book is of inestimable value and distinguishes such books from ephemeral literature" (Thompson, 2005, "Classics: Mentors on Paper" section, ¶ 3). Additionally, classics help gifted students connect with people and places across the continents and across time and help students "to know the mind of the world . . . hear the song of their species" (Thompson, 2001). In addition to thematic considerations, the classics provide vocabulary and syntax that challenge and expand the verbal facilities of even the most advanced students.

> "Some books are undeservedly forgotten; none are undeservedly remembered."
>
> —W. H. Auden

The Junior Great Books (JGB) program provides outstanding text selections and a training program that helps group facilitators (teachers, librarians, or parents) engage students in high-level discussion using the Shared Inquiry Method

> to instill the habits of mind that characterize a self-reliant thinker, reader, and learner. . . . [P]articipants search for answers to fundamental questions raised by a text. This search is inherently active; it involves taking what the author has given us and trying to grasp its full meaning, to interpret or reach an understanding of the text in light of our experience and using sound reasoning. . . . Participants gain experience in communicating complex ideas and in supporting, testing, and expanding their own thoughts . . . promotes thoughtful dialogue and open debate. (Great Books Foundation, 2003, ¶ 1)

Discussion revolves around three key types of questions: factual, evaluative, and interpretive. The program has obvious value

Themed Junior Great Books for Middle School

Wide Open Spaces: American Frontiers
To Be a Hero
And Justice for All
What on Earth? An Ecology Reader
A House Divided: America's Civil War
Echoes From Mt. Olympus
The Harlem Renaissance
From There to Here: The Immigrant Experience
Dark Days: America's Great Depression
Times of Change: Vietnam and the '60s

Themed Junior Great Books for High School

Nature of Life: Readings in Biology
Keeping Things Whole: Readings in Environmental Science
Will of the People: Readings in American Democracy
A Latino National Conversation: Readings on Assimilation
The Soul of the Text: An Anthology of Jewish Literature

for gifted students, and the inherent structures and process will be familiar to most teachers of the gifted and English/language arts specialists. JGB materials can be part of a required curriculum, the core of a pull-out gifted program, or part of an after-school group at the school or public library.

In recent years, JGB has expanded its text offerings to include themed collections for both middle and high school that may be of great value to gifted middle school students and their teachers. The traditional JGB anthologies include a range of challenging selections from different genres, with the unifying connection of challenging reading level and universal themes that lend themselves to open-ended questioning. In addition to their use in reading, language arts, and gifted resource room classes, the newer themed books provide excellent sources for differentiating instruction in the content areas, whether the class is honors-level or heterogeneously grouped. These may also fit well with middle school interdisciplinary units and themes that often lack the depth and complexity gifted students need. The high school volumes offer significant challenge and advanced content for gifted middle school students, and both levels address topics and themes commonly found in secondary curricula.

Baskin (1998), however, cautioned that JGB and its Shared Inquiry Method may be too dependent on "the intelligence and ability of teachers who are often untrained in individualizing work for the intellectually gifted" (p. 69). Additionally, she suggested that the use of JGB with gifted students might benefit from expanding and varying the routine to include more student-centered and student-directed opportunities. Some possibilities might include reader's theater or other dramatic interpretations, writing alternative endings, character collages, and creating and performing ballads or raps.

Regardless of the specific advanced materials selected, instruction for gifted readers should emphasize critical reading and advanced skills. Students should explore the moral ambiguities and social issues to which they are especially sensitive. Baskin (1998) also suggested the following objectives:

- develop inferential and prediction strategies and schemas for anticipating meaning;
- use scholarly methods of inquiry;
- develop awareness of literary devices and use them in writing;
- develop sensitivity to symbols and other abstract story-telling devices;
- identify and critique rationales for decision making and consequences of choices; and
- draw analogies between fictional themes and contemporary issues.

A variety of excellent language arts/reading-based materials are available from the College of William and Mary's Center for Gifted Education (see http://cfge.wm.edu/curriculum.php). Some are interdisciplinary units with strong reading/writing content such as *Persuasion, Utopia*, or *The 1940s*. Novel study guides for advanced readers called "Navigators" include many common middle school titles.

Balancing required/assigned reading and guided independent reading offers students both a private relationship with books and a public opportunity for discussion with their intellectual peers. The responsibility for this reader's advisory process should be shared by parents, teachers, counselors, and librarians. Because middle schools span a wide age range, and might include any configuration of fifth through ninth grade, it is important for adults to select or recommend books only after thoughtful consideration of students' maturity and ability.

Community context must also be considered. Some titles will be controversial and disruptive (with regard to politics, language, violence, religion, portrayal of social issues, etc.) to some children and in some schools and communities, but not in others. Thus, it is essential that teachers actually read the books! It is not enough to rely on dust jacket blurbs, reviews, or student opinions. Young adult literature has come a long way from the Hardy Boys and Nancy Drew, and while this makes for a vibrant and exciting range of choices, it can also challenge more traditional sensibilities. It is also important to weigh whether a book should be available for individual independent reading or should be assigned to everyone in a class.

Certain books are more likely to appeal to gifted middle school readers, though there are, of course, no hard and fast rules that guarantee a book's success. However, there are books that specifically address the needs, interests, and concerns of gifted middle school students and their abilities to read for depth, inference, implication, and application to their own unique perspective and life situations. While girls of this age are willing to read books with both male and female protagonists, finding books to challenge and engage boys is often more difficult. Hébert (1995) suggested that biographies can help gifted male students find helpful insights into dealing with their problems, and some of these are included in the lists that follow. The therapeutic value of biographies and the role models they provide has been supported at least as far back as the pioneering work of Leta Hollingworth (1942). In Silverman's book *Counseling the Gifted and Talented* (2000), Jerry Flack and Deirdre Lovecky have compiled a more complete list of biographies that can be used with gifted students.

Overall, the choice of books for gifted students, whether for developmental bibliotherapy or other purposes, should be guided by several key principles (Baskin, 1998; Kerr, 1991):

1. Books should be good literature, whether targeted at young adults, children, or adults.
2. Books should be concerned with gifted people, though they do not necessarily have to address giftedness specifically as a central issue.
3. Books should have characters, themes, and conflicts with which gifted readers can identify.
4. Language in the books should be rich, varied, accurate, and complex, including use of dialect and language patterns that are unusual or from other eras and cultures.
5. Books should emphasize theme over plot, including philosophical, moral, and social issues.
6. Books with complex structural components such as time manipulations, parallel plots, interdisciplinary content, multiple narrators, and varying points of view engage gifted readers.
7. Books should include a wide variety of genres, including nonfiction, unusual reference materials, humor, drama, biography and autobiography, and poetry.

Connecting Students With Books

In order for the reading experience of selected books to have the desired impact, there must be some structured follow-up by an interested adult. Regular book conferences, teacher-student interactive reading journals, or group discussion sessions offer interactions that support and expand students' reading experiences. It isn't enough to hand the students the book, let them read it on their own, and then move on.

Even when students do independent reading with completely self-selected titles, it is important for them to have conversations with interested adults who can probe, question, and extend thinking and evaluation, as well as opportunities to talk with peers about what they are reading. Many of us who participate in adult book clubs find that, after the discussion of the assigned title, far-ranging discussion of other books people are reading uncover new authors, titles, topics, and ideas. When adolescents suggest titles to each other, books they're excited about or "couldn't put down," the social connections that are made may encourage other students to read the same books. Since it's often not "cool" in middle school to discuss books you loved or books that kept you up late finishing, structuring such conversations in classrooms and resource rooms opens the door for avid readers. They can share their passions in a safe and supportive environment that is nurtured and watched over by sensitive and caring teachers who also value reading and readers.

This classroom climate issue is critical. Gifted readers must feel that they are not deviants because of their excitement about ideas, their mature or sophisticated means of expression, their deeper and more intense questioning, and their passion for and interest in reading. Too often, they are used as models or tutors in reading classes without opportunities for their own growth. Instead, they need the opportunity to engage with others who offer challenge and debate at the same level; otherwise, they become arrogant (from always being the top student in the class or group) and lazy (from being able to gain high grades without any real work).

As part of the gifted English/language arts curriculum at Beachwood Middle School in Ohio, each interdisciplinary unit in the 2-year curriculum I designed had an extended list of correlated books for independent reading. While the class was supposedly homogeneous, there was a wide range of reading abilities and interests among the gifted students. The lists I compiled in collaboration with the school librarian included fiction and nonfiction, as well as both classic and young adult titles.

Culminating projects were required that provided opportunities for students to use a variety of creative approaches to share their understanding and appreciation of their book, as well as to demonstrate its connection to the unit theme. These almost always extended beyond the traditional book report and expanded students' abilities to give presentations and share their knowledge. The following example is a sampling of the supplemental independent reading list from my seventh- and eighth-grade unit on the brain/mind. Especially with nonfiction titles, it is important to update the list continually in order to keep up with current research and new publications. Because it was part of the first unit in the school year, the culminating project was written. Later projects allowed for more creative responses.

The Mind: Guided Reading List

This list includes a variety of fiction and nonfiction books on the brain, the mind, human psychology and personality, intelligence, and coping with emotional and psychological problems. Your written report of approximately 3–5 typed pages is due on _____ and will include answers to the following:

Fiction
1. Write a brief (no more than half a page!) plot summary including the ending.

2. Discuss the psychological, intellectual, and emotional issues involved and their effect on the individual, the family, and the surroundings.
3. What help or support was available? Who gave it or didn't give it? Did it work? How and why?
4. Your response to the reading (emotional and personal, as well as intellectual and evaluative.)
5. Other questions and comments of interest to you.

Nonfiction
1. Write a brief (no more than one page!) content overview.
2. What were the most important things you learned from this book? Be specific. In what ways has your understanding of human thinking, feeling, and behavior changed as a result of reading this book?
3. What treatments or approaches are available for the problems described? What are the unanswered questions that still remain?
4. Your response to the reading (emotional and personal, as well as intellectual and evaluative.)
5. Other questions and comments of interest to you.

Nonfiction Titles (* titles are adult-level reading)

101 Questions Your Brain Has Asked About Itself But Couldn't Answer Until Now by Faith Hickman Brynie

Bringing Up Parents: The Teenager's Handbook by Alex J. Packer

*Dibs in Search of Self** by Virginia Axline

*Smart Girls: A New Psychology of Girls, Women, and Giftedness** by Barbara Kerr

Perfectionism: What's Bad About Being Too Good by Miriam Adderholdt-Elliott

Living in the Labyrinth: A Personal Journey Through the Maze of Alzheimer's by Diana McGowin
> The author was only 45 when she began experiencing the symptoms of Alzheimer's Disease.

How to Improve Your Memory by Dan Halacy

Girl, Interrupted by Susanna Kaysen
> A memoir of the author's stay in a mental institution.

Fiction Titles (* titles are adult-level reading)

The Drowning Boy by Susan Terris
> 12-year-old Jason considers himself a failure. He is forced to the brink of suicide by an unsympathetic family.

The Boy Who Could Make Himself Disappear by Kim Platt
> A poignant description of a 12-year-old boy's tragic journey into schizophrenia.

Born of the Sun by Gillian Cross
> Paula's father's actions become increasingly disturbing while on an exploration of the mountains of Peru.

I Never Promised You a Rose Garden by Hanna Greene (Joanne Greenburg)
> A young girl is put into a mental hospital by her parents with hope of a successful recovery from her dual life in both reality and a world of fantasy voices.

Reading contracts can also guide students' reading, whether in nonfiction or fiction. Contracts should delineate what is to be read, a timeline for completion, checkpoints with the teacher, and a final outcome. These can be negotiated as part of or in place of the standard reading/language arts curriculum. Since grade-level basal readers are often too fragmented or simplistic for gifted and advanced readers, reading contracts can provide a vibrant alternative, keeping students engaged in and excited about reading throughout their adolescence. Here, too, teachers need to guide the process and ensure that critical reading and interpretation are taking place, including students' understanding of the author's style, appreciating varied examples of syntax and diction, and mastering advanced vocabulary.

Another common approach for gifted students is an author study project. Whether focused on a young adult author (e.g., Paul Zindel, S. E. Hinton, Robert Cormier, Stephanie Tolan, Richard Peck), popular adult writer (e.g., Stephen King, J. R. R. Tolkien, Maya Angelou, Annie Dillard, John Grisham), or a classic author (e.g., John Steinbeck, Jack London, Emily Dickinson, Pearl Buck), students have the opportunity to study style, recurrent themes, and the impact of an author's life experiences on his or her writing, as well as to be introduced to literary criticism and reviews. These projects can incorporate research skills with reading and expand students' understanding of writers and the writing process. They can also focus on important writers in scientific and technical fields (e.g., Isaac Asimov) or in the arts (e.g., Paul Klee). The important thing is that students are reading, writing, and thinking about people and topics that interest them and expand their minds.

Teachers can also encourage reading and connect students with books through reading aloud. While some might consider this too "elementary" for middle school students, I have found that students listen intently and respond strongly when the right selections or books are chosen. Reading important or provocative passages or even whole chapters can provide opportunities for group discussion of characters and issues. At the start of the school year, Richard Peck's short story "Priscilla and the Wimps" (which can be found in Gallo, 1984) is a great read-aloud to begin discussion of bullying and intimidation. Often used as a significant element in booktalking (a librarian's essential tool for introducing students to books), reading aloud can whet students' interest in a particular title or author. It can also introduce new forms such as poetry, graphic novels, memoirs, or picture books. One example of a rich and unusual picture book is Kathryn Lasky and Christopher Knight's rainforest photo essay *The Most Beautiful Roof in the World*, which could also connect effectively with common interdisciplinary units on ecosystems and ecology.

Both *Willie Was Different* by Norman Rockwell and *Annabelle Swift, Kindergartner* by Amy Schwartz are children's books that could be read aloud to safely open up discussion about the "perils" of being gifted. Either would provide excellent introductions to S. E. Hinton's *The Outsiders* or other more mature titles on alienation and isolation. Another personal favorite is *The Three Questions*, a children's book based on a story by Leo Tolstoy and written and illustrated by Jon J. Muth. The three questions—"What is the best time to do things?," "Who is the most important one?," and "What is the right thing to do?"—are essential philosophical and moral inquiry for readers at all levels.

Most middle schools require summer and vacation reading. Lists provided for students should be designed to keep them reading over the summer; therefore, the books included on them should be of high-interest. Summer reading is usually followed by some kind of in-school project or follow-up, often to give teachers an idea of students' abilities and attitudes at the very start of the school year and to build a common starting point for English classes. Students share their projects or reports, have tests on the books, collaborate to create bulletin boards, and so forth. However, these summer reading lists are often too easy for gifted readers.

Again, at Beachwood Middle School, we addressed this issue by appending a "Challenge List" to our summer reading brochure. The list was compiled by the gifted resource teacher, the English teachers, and the librarian. While all students could select titles from this list, gifted students (and their families) were informed that they were *required* to read at least one title from this list. These choices included more classics, were at a more advanced reading level, and dealt with issues that were potentially of more interest to gifted students. The books were also often longer and more complex in literary structure.

While all students in the school completed the same type of project, the in-class follow-up for students in the gifted program differed. Balancing all-school activities with targeted appropriate activities for gifted students is part of the juggling that occurs when successfully blending middle school and gifted programming. The gifted students at Beachwood Middle School were able to feel part of the school while engaging with materials at a more appropriate level. The follow-up in the gifted class allowed for in-depth critical discussion and book sharing, but for observers looking at all the projects hanging in the hallways throughout the school, gifted students' work was blended seamlessly with that of the rest of the student body.

One of my most successful spring break reading projects provided students with a list of short classics (e.g., John Steinbeck's *The Red Pony*, Ernest Hemingway's *The Old Man and the Sea*) from which they had to select one. A list of choices for follow-up projects was organized by Gardner's multiple intelligences, and students had to choose one. My favorite student products included the reading aloud of key passages from Pearl S. Buck's *The Good Earth* to a soundtrack of carefully chosen heavy metal music and the student's explanation of why they were thematically connected (musical intelligence); a pair of limericks that precisely captured *The Old Man and the Sea* (verbal-linguistic intelligence); and an oil painting of the house from Edgar Allan Poe's *The Fall of the House of Usher* (visual-spatial). Since that time, Jacquelyn Glasgow has created a useful project guide (*Using Young Adult Literature: Thematic Activities Based on Gardner's Multiple Intelligences*, 2002) that could be applied to various literary experiences.

Some schools have required reading courses, especially for all sixth graders, regardless of ability. Other schools may offer mini-courses for advanced students, such as a course called "Between the Lines" offered at middle schools in the Cleveland Heights-University Heights schools (see sidebar on the next page). The strategies described above and the titles that follow can fit a variety of middle school classes and organizational patterns.

Books to Use With Gifted Middle School Students

Schroeder-Davis (1992) examined more than 200 examples of realistic fiction "about" gifted children and identified 10 relevant themes:

- multipotentiality;
- a mentor relationship;
- physical isolation;
- a desire for autonomy;
- psychological isolation;
- intensity and exclusivity of focus;
- coercive egalitarianism;
- heightened sensitivity and awareness;
- perfectionism; and
- familiar and/or peer rivalry.

The complete bibliography he created, which is available from the Minnesota Council for the Gifted and Talented, consists of an annotated book list for early elementary through high school students. Other sources for extended annotated lists include *Books for the Gifted Child* (Baskin & Harris, 1980) and *Some of My Best Friends Are Books: Guiding Gifted Readers from Preschool to High School* (Halsted, 2002). While not specifically targeted for gifted readers, the American Library Association's (ALA) annual list of Best Books for Young Adults, the National Council of Teachers

Between the Lines

"Between the Lines" is a literature-based class for sixth and seventh graders. The class meets once a week for 80 minutes throughout the school year. We have created a 2-year cycle of literary selections to ensure that sixth graders don't repeat the same material the following year. Of course, selections may be added or deleted due to student interest and ability levels or teacher discovery.

Some titles are read by all members of the group, and students who finish quickly are provided additional books (by the same author, on the same theme, of the same genre, etc.). In addition, the teachers spend one-to-one time with individual students providing reader's advisory and bibliocounseling to match just the right book with just the right reader at just the right time.

The class was created to foster the development of students' abilities to analyze and interpret the literary works of various writers and artists and provide opportunities to go beyond the standard English curriculum. The diverse selections encourage students to share opinions, make inferences, formulate judgments, and promote growth of their critical thinking skills and strategies. Through the use of novels, short stories, plays, poetry, folk tales, and essays, students are able to read, discuss, and form conclusions regarding the selections. Writers' Workshops are included periodically to provide opportunities to generate individual or group creative projects. In the past, we have also utilized film excerpts and song lyrics to emphasize unique or recurring themes and authors' styles and life experiences to provide further opportunities for thoughtful discussions.

—Kathy Pahys, gifted resource teacher,
Roxboro Middle School, Cleveland Heights, OH

of English (NCTE) books *Your Reading: A Booklist for Junior High and Middle School Students* (Nilson, 1991) and *Books for You: A Booklist for Senior High Students* (Wurth, 1992), and the ALA's annual list of Newberry Award winners (see http://www. ala.org/ala/alsc/awardsscholarships/literaryawds/newberymedal/ newberymedal.htm) also provide up-to-date titles that might well serve gifted students during middle school. Silverman (2000) also provides a list of books for children featuring gifted children and a list of biographies for gifted students in her book on counseling the gifted and talented. Thomas Hébert has also provided useful lists, though these span ages from preschool through high school: "The Right Books for Bright Girls at the Right Times" and "The Right Books for Bright Boys at the Right Times."

There are many titles that are specifically appropriate for gifted middle school students that could have been on these lists of books. The following will provide a solid start:

Titles for Younger Middle School Gifted Students

A Single Shard by Linda Sue Park
The Great Whale of Kansas by Richard W. Jennings
Buried Onions by Gary Soto
Go and Come Back by Joan Abelove
Aria of the Sea by Dia Calhoun
Kids on Strike by Susan Campbell Bartoletti
The Music of Dolphins by Karen Hesse
Red Scarf Girl by Ji-li Jiang
Moves Make the Man by Bruce Brooks
Cheating Lessons by Nan Willard Cappo
The Outcasts of 19 Schuyler Place or *The View From Saturday* by E.
    L. Konigsburg
The World's Greatest Expert on Absolutely Everything Is Crying by
    Barbara Bottner
Midnight Hour Encores by Bruce Brooks
A Room Made of Windows by Eleanor Cameron

Make Lemonade and *True Believer* (the first two books in the Lemonade series) by Virginia Euwer Wolff

And This Is Laura by Ellen Conford

Among Friends or *Twenty Pageants Later* by Caroline Cooney

Ordinary Jack by Helen Cresswell

Bilgewater by Jane Gardam

Ordinary Genius: The Story of Albert Einstein by Stephanie S. McPherson

Treasures of the Morrow by H. M. Hoover

Very Far Away From Anywhere Else by Ursula LeGuin

The Facts and Fictions of Minna Pratt by Patricia MacLachlan

In Summer Light by Zibby Oneal

Words by Heart by Ouida Sebestyen

The Mozart Season by Virginia Euwer Wolff

Fast Talk on a Slow Track by Rita Williams-Garcia

No Safe Harbors, *Welcome to the Ark*, *Flight of the Raven*, and *Surviving the Applewhites* by Stephanie S. Tolan

Simon Pure by Julian F. Thompson

I Hate Being Gifted by Patricia Hermes

Libby on Wednesday by Zilpha Keatley Snyder

When No One Was Looking by Rosemary Wells

The Golden Compass by Philip Pullman

The Friends by Rosa Guy

Remembering the Good Times by Richard Peck

Tell Me if the Lovers Are Losers by Cynthia Voigt

The Great Interactive Dream Machine by Richard Peck

The Schernoff Discoveries by Gary Paulsen

Misfits by James Howe

Ender's Game and *Ender's Shadow* by Orson Scott Card

Ella Minnow Pea by Mark Dunn

Titles for Older Middle School Gifted Students

The Invisible Ladder: An Anthology of Contemporary American Poems for Young Readers edited by Liz Rosenberg

Are You Alone on Purpose? by Nancy Werlin

Clan of the Cave Bear by Jean Auel

Brimstone Journals by Ron Koertge

A Separate Peace by John Knowles

The Mark of Conte by Sonia Leviten

Been Clever Forever by Bruce Stone

Eva by Peter Dickinson

A Bone From a Dry Sea by Peter Dickinson

Winning the Gold by Bart Conner

Parallel Times: Growing Up in Black and White by Brent Staples

Gifted Hands: The Ben Carson Story by Ben Carson, with Cecil Murphy

A Circle of Friends by Maeve Binchy

Staying Fat for Sarah Byrnes by Chris Crutcher

Breaking Barriers: A Memoir by Carl T. Rowan

Voices in the Mirror: An Autobiography by Gordon Parks

The Child Buyer by John Hersey

Firestarter by Stephen King

Whirligig by Paul Fleischman

Mango Elephants in the Sun by Susana Herrera

Running Tough: Memoirs of a Football Maverick by Tony Dorsett

My Brilliant Career by Miles Franklin

Shizuko's Daughter by Kyoko Mori

Every Time a Rainbow Dies by Rita Williams-Garcia

The Ropemaker by Peter Dickinson

Nonfiction Books About and for Gifted Kids

The Gifted Kids' Survival Guide: A Teen Handbook by Judy Galbraith and Jim Delisle

Girls and Young Women Leading the Way: 20 True Stories About Leadership by Frances A. Karnes and Suzanne M. Bean

When Gifted Kids Don't Have All the Answers: How to Meet Their Social and Emotional Needs by Jim Delisle and Judy Galbraith

Perfectionism: What's Bad About Being Too Good? (Revised and Updated Edition) by Miriam Adderholdt and Jan Goldberg

A Hope in the Unseen: An American Odyssey From the Inner City to the Ivy League by Ron Suskind

Quirky List of Texts
for the English/Language Arts Classroom

These books are listed separately because of their structure, theme, language, and/or literary merit. I have found them particularly useful tools for covering the standard literary components of most middle school curricular guides, and they are especially suitable for discussion with gifted students. These books were read as a whole group in my honors English/gifted class (unless students had already read them). Even a simple book (like Ron Jones' *The Acorn People*) has given rise to important discussion about people's differences and our responsibilities to each other. Interestingly, in our school, this book was taught in both the gifted language arts class (as part of an interdisciplinary unit on human diversity) and in the remedial reading class (because it is short and easy to read). The differences were in pace (the gifted students read it in a weekend, while the struggling readers took several weeks) and the follow-up questions and activities.

For novels like William Golding's *Lord of the Flies*, the difference between typical and gifted students is often in the timing; typical students may read this as part of a high school English class, while gifted students are ready to grapple with the length, language, and themes in middle school. Many other titles could be on this list, and in some cases, thoughtful articulation with high school honors classes is necessary to avoid repetition and conflict. But, for teachers looking for a starting point, here are some suggestions:

Call of the Wild by Jack London
The Giver by Lois Lowry
The Chocolate War by Robert Cormier

The Outsiders by S. E. Hinton
Lord of the Flies by William Golding
The Acorn People by Ron Jones
Flowers for Algernon by Daniel Keyes
Nothing But the Truth by Avi
To Kill a Mockingbird by Harper Lee
Of Mice and Men by John Steinbeck
The Hobbit by J. R. R. Tolkien
Catcher in the Rye by J. D. Salinger
The Pearl by John Steinbeck
I Am the Cheese by Robert Cormier

Movies as Cinematherapy

It would seem a serious omission not to at least mention movies as a "cinematherapeutic tool" for gifted students. Movies like *Little Man Tate* (1991), *Searching for Bobby Fischer* (1993), *Good Will Hunting* (1997), *October Sky* (1999), *Finding Forrester* (2000), and *The Incredibles* (2004) provide rich characters and conflicts, as well as fictional peers and mentors. Numerous episodes of *The Simpsons* explore the personality traits of, and issues faced by Lisa Simpson, the perennially misunderstood and underappreciated gifted sister. An excellent source for movie suggestions about gifted children and issues is Hoagie's Gifted Education Page on Movies Featuring Gifted Kids (and Adults!) (http://www.hoagiesgifted.org/movies.htm). Watching such films make excellent parent night activities or parent/student evenings with either combined or separate discussions to follow.

Conclusion

Books and the development of sophisticated reading abilities are powerful, essential tools to enhance the academic achievement, cognitive powers, and social/emotional awareness of gifted students. The general education curriculum and classroom are rarely adequate for this task, thus advanced differentiated strategies and materials are necessary. The booklists, materials, and strategies described in this chapter can serve as a guide for teachers, parents, and librarians.

Next Steps . . . Taking Action

1. Use all available data to identify gifted students and others who are advanced readers.

2. Use a variety of grouping approaches and programs, both in and out of the English/language arts classroom, to provide appropriately challenging reading instruction and literary experiences that are both interest- and ability-based.

3. Use bibliotherapy and reader's advisory to match students with books that help them meet other gifted people, explore social/emotional issues, and investigate personal problem-solving strategies.

4. Research available resources that complement existing curricula. Blend both required reading and independent reading with a variety of individual and group reader-response activities that develop high-level critical reading, thinking, and analysis.

References

Baskin, B. (1998). Call me Ishmael: A look at gifted middle school readers. In K. Beers & B. G. Samuels (Eds.), *Into focus: Understanding and creating middle school readers* (pp. 65–78). Norwood, MA: Christopher-Gordon.

Baskin, B. H., & Harris, K. H. (1980). *Books for the gifted child.* New York: R. R. Bowker.

Delisle, J., & Galbraith, J. (2002). *When gifted kids don't have all the answers: How to meet their social and emotional needs.* Minneapolis, MN: Free Spirit.

Gallo, D. R. (Ed.). (1984). *Sixteen: Short stories by outstanding writers for young adults.* New York: Dell.

Glasgow, J. (2002). *Using young adult literature: Thematic activities based on Gardner's multiple intelligences.* Norwood, MA: Christopher-Gordon.

Great Books Foundation. (2003). *Our educational philosophy: The shared inquiry method of learning.* Retrieved May 19, 2005, from http://www.greatbooks.org/programs/junior/philosophy/sharinq.shtml

Halsted, J. W. (2002). *Some of my best friends are books: Guiding gifted readers from preschool to high school* (2nd ed.). Scottsdale, AZ: Great Potential Press.

Hébert, T. P. (1995). Using biography to counsel gifted young men. *Journal of Secondary Gifted Education, 6,* 208–219.

Hébert, T. P., & Kent, R. (2000). Nurturing social and emotional development in gifted teenagers through young adult literature. *Roeper Review, 22,* 167–71.

Herz, S. K., & Gallo, D. R. (1996). *From Hinton to Hamlet: Building bridges between young adult literature and the classics.* Westport, CO: Greenwood Press.

Hollingworth, L. S. (1942). *Children above 180 IQ Stanford-Binet: Origin and development.* Yonkers-on-Hudson, NY: World Book.

Hynes, A. M., & Hynes-Berry, M. (1987). *Biblio/poetry therapy: The interactive process: A handbook.* Boulder, CO: Westview Press.

Jackson, A. W., & Davis, G. A. (2000). *Turning points 2000: Educating adolescents in the 21st century.* New York: Teachers College Press.

Kerr, B. A. (1991). *A handbook for counseling the gifted and talented.* Alexandria, VA: American Counseling Association.

Reis, S. M. (2001). What can we do with talented readers? *Teaching for High Potential, 3*(1), 1–2.

Reis, S. M., Gubbins, E. J., & Richards, S. (2002). *Meeting the needs of talented readers: SEM-R.* Storrs: National Research Center on the Gifted and Talented, University of Connecticut. Retrieved May 19, 2005, from http://www.gifted.uconn.edu/extras/semr.pdf

Renzulli, J. S. (1997). *Interest-A-Lyzer family of instruments: A manual for teachers.* Mansfield Center, CT: Creative Learning Press.

Reynales, B. (1978). Preventive bibliotherapy for the older adolescent: An overview. *Phi Delta Gamma Journal, 18,* 110–117.

Richards, S. (2001). Using books to spark and ignite students' interests. *Teaching for High Potential, 3*(1), 4.

Schroeder-Davis, S. (1992). *The gifted child in contemporary fiction: An annotated bibliography.* Minneapolis, MN: Minnesota Council for the Gifted and Talented.

Silverman, L. K. (2000). *Counseling the gifted and talented.* Denver, CO: Love.

Slavin, R. E. (1999). *Technical proposal: Design, development, and testing of comprehensive school reform models.* Baltimore, MD: Success for All Foundation.

Thompson, M. (2001, December 7). *Language arts: The core of all content.* Keynote speech at the annual meeting of the Texas Association for the Gifted and Talented, San Antonio.

Thompson, M. (2005). *Developing verbal talent.* Retrieved May 19, 2005, from http://www.ctd.northwestern.edu/resources/talentdev/verbaltalent.html

Tomlinson, C. A. (1992). Gifted education and the middle school movement: Two voices on teaching the academically talented. *Journal for the Education for the Gifted, 15,* 206–238.

Vacca, J. A., Vacca, R. T., & Gove, M. K. (1991). *Reading and learning to read.* New York: Harper Collins.

Wurth, S. (Ed.). (1992). *Books for you: A booklist for senior high students.* Urbana, IL: National Council of Teachers of English.

Additional Resources

Austin, P. (2003, April/May). Challenging gifted readers. *Book Links*, 32–37.

Flack, J., & Lamb, P. (1984, September/October). Making use of gifted characters in literature. *G/C/T,* 3–11.

Frank, A. J., & McBee, M. T. (2003). The use of *Harry Potter and the Sorcerer's Stone* to discuss identity development with gifted adolescents. *Journal of Secondary Gifted Education, 15,* 33–38.

Frasier, M., & McCannon, C. (1981). Using bibliotherapy with gifted children. *Gifted Child Quarterly, 25,* 81–85.

Levande, D. (1999). Gifted readers and reading instruction. *California Association for the Gifted (CAG) Communicator, 30*(1). Retrieved June 25, 2005, from http://www.hoagiesgifted.org/levande.htm

Milne, H., & Reis, S. M. (2000). Using videotherapy to address the social and emotional needs of gifted children. *Gifted Child Today, 23*(1), 24–29.

Nilsen, A. P. (Ed.). (1991). *Your reading: A booklist for junior high and middle school students.* Urbana, IL: National Council of Teachers of English.

Olenchak, F. R. (2001). When gifted readers hunt for books. *Voices from the Middle, 9*(2), 71–73.

Parker, J. P. (1989). *Instructional strategies for teaching the gifted.* Boston: Allyn and Bacon.

Rakow, S. R. (1991). Young adult literature for honors students? *English Journal, 80*(1), 48–51.

Schlichter, C. L., & Burke, M. (1994). Using books to nurture the social and emotional development of gifted students. *Roeper Review, 16,* 280–283.

Smutny, J. F. (2001). *Creative strategies for teaching language arts to gifted students (K–8)* (ERIC Digest #E612). Reston, VA: ERIC Clearinghouse on Disabilities and Gifted Education.

Competitions,
Talent Searches,
Summer Programs,
and Community Service

Essential Questions

1. How might gifted middle school students benefit from participation in competitions, summer programs, and other outside-of-school learning experiences?

2. What opportunities are available to extend students' learning beyond the limits of the middle school calendar, building, and daily schedule?

Clubs, competitions, Saturday and summer programs, and community service all extend gifted students' learning experiences beyond the school day and year, beyond their geographic area and immediate peer group, and into the larger society. Involvement in these activities can result in greater social interactions with like-minded individuals of all ages, as well as increased knowledge in specific areas of interest and passion. Students may also discover and explore new interests, which contributes to academic growth and a broader background before high school and college (Brody & Stanley, 1991; Piskurich, 2003). Characteristics and benefits of advanced out-of-school programs also include a faster pace, higher conceptual levels, specially prepared teachers with higher level expectations, opportunities for in-depth research and evaluation, and clarification and confirmation of an individual student's gifts and talents (Feldhusen, 1991). Students may use summer and online coursework for academic acceleration, which might allow them to take more challenging courses during the school year and potentially enter college early. After-school clubs and competitions, as well as enrichment courses, also put students in contact with more students of like ability who share their interests.

National talent searches provide opportunities for middle school students to take the ACT or SAT—tests that are designed for high school students. Students' scores and norming information for the tests contextualize and identify students' advanced levels of performance. The drawbacks of these instruments are that they are less likely to identify gifted girls than gifted boys and they may be biased against low-income and minority children. Some students may also find the experience stressful, rather than challenging. The advantage is that students' patterns of strength and weakness emerge and provide the foundation for decisions on advanced classes and school summer programs.

Talent searches are followed up at centers such as the Johns Hopkins University Center for Talented Youth (CTY), the Duke University Talent Identification Program (TIP), and Northwestern University's Center for Talent Development (CTD). They provide challenging courses, as well as educational and career counseling, to students who have performed well on the talent search instruments.

While children may have taken extra lessons and classes in many different areas (e.g., drama, music, science, computer) in elementary school, by middle school there is a danger of over-scheduling. Young adolescents need free time to relax, read, listen to music, and talk with friends. There is always the risk of well-intentioned adults offering gifted adolescents too many choices and opportunities that can overwhelm them and unwittingly play into their perfectionist tendencies. Students with multipotentiality may feel they have to attempt to do it all, thus it is important to help middle school students narrow their focus and choose activities that have the most individual impact and meaning.

Clubs and Competitions

Many gifted students enjoy the camaraderie and challenge of individual and group academic competitions and clubs. Participation in school- or community-sponsored chess clubs, creative writing groups, library book clubs, and science clubs can provide "academic intramurals" that offer many of the interpersonal benefits of competitions without the pressure.

Whether as part of a gifted class curriculum, as an after-school activity, or as part of a pull-out program, students involved in contests socialize with intellectual peers and those with similar interests in a combined cooperative and competitive environment. Students experience academic challenges in formats that differ from what can be typically offered in the classroom, and many of these challenges provide opportunities for establishing better interpersonal, problem-solving, and teamwork skills. Self-esteem and confidence are developed as students engage in healthy competition under the guidance of encouraging and supportive adult coaches. In addition, artistic contests provide opportunities for valuable feedback and possible awards. Some academic competitions also open up other opportunities and offer scholarships or other recognition and awards for schools and individuals. Two resources provide extensive lists of competitions, though not necessarily targeted solely for middle school students: *Competitions for Talented Kids* (Karnes & Riley, 2005) lists more than 140 competitions in various categories such as language arts, engineering, leadership, science, and technology, and the National Honor Society's Web site (http://www.nhs.us/scaa/SCAA_List.cfm) also lists competitions sponsored by various government, college, service, and corporate entities, some of which are open to middle school students.

The following list, however, is a select group of experiences particularly appropriate for middle school students. Though this is by no means a "definitive" compilation, it is a good place to start.

Destination ImagiNation
http://www.destinationimagination.org

Destination ImagiNation is a team-based state, national, and international organization that uses creative problem-solving scenarios to teach life skills and expand imagination. It helps students build confidence and develop skills in teamwork, brainstorming, project and time management, creative and critical thinking, collaboration and presentation, and research.

FIRST LEGO League Robotics
http://www.firstlegoleague.org

This international program for children ages 9–14 combines a hands-on, interactive robotics program with a sports-like atmosphere. Teams consisting of up to 10 players receive a new challenge each September, and they have 8 weeks to create a fully autonomous robot using the LEGO MIND-STORMS technology. The robot must be able to complete various missions of the FLL International "Robot Game." Students develop skills in team building, problem solving, creativity, and analytical thinking. As part of the process, students also receive a "Research Assignment" that relates to a current world problem or opportunity. They must develop a responsive presentation after searching the Internet, talking to scientists, and visiting the library.

National Engineers Week Future City Competition
http://www.futurecity.org

This educational engineering program sponsored by National Engineers Week is for seventh- and eighth-grade students who must work together in teams to present their vision of a city of the future. Students work together with teachers and engineer mentors from the community, in the process developing skills in teamwork, communication, practical applications of math and science, computer use, and problem solving.

Future Problem Solving Program
http://www.fpsp.org

Like Destination ImagiNation and Odyssey of the Mind, this program uses a team approach. Students develop problem-solving, communication, research, and teamwork skills while actively and optimistically exploring the problems of the future and developing and presenting creative solutions. Competitions are at the state, national, and international levels.

National Geographic Bee
http://www.nationalgeographic.com/geographybee

This contest is designed and sponsored by the National Geographic Society to encourage teachers to include geography in their classrooms, spark student interest in the subject, and increase public awareness about geography. Schools with students in grades 4–8 are eligible for this challenging test of geographic knowledge.

The Knowledge Master Open
http://www.greatauk.com/KMO.html

Teams of students compete from their own classrooms in a computer-based academic challenge using curriculum-based content questions. Challenging and low-cost, there are competitions at grades 5/6 and 7/8.

MATHCOUNTS
http://www.mathcounts.org

MATHCOUNTS is a national math enrichment, coaching, and competition program that promotes middle school mathematics achievement. Students compete individually or as part of a team. Competitions are written and oral and are held in schools first, after which local winners proceed to state and national competitions. MATHCOUNTS challenges students' math skills and develops their self-confidence.

Model United Nations

Offered by many states and regional entities, Model United Nations simulations help students learn about international relations and gain understanding of various countries and cultures. Students develop skills in communication, negotiation tactics, and conflict prevention and resolution. Many useful materials are available from the U.S. State Department.

Midwest Academic Talent Search

http://www.ctd.northwestern.edu/mats/description.html

The Midwest Academic Talent Search uses well-known college admissions tests (the ACT and the SAT), as well as the EXPLORE test (designed for third through sixth graders), to provide a view of the mathematical and verbal abilities of talented sixth through ninth graders. After testing, students and parents receive information about specialized curricula, enrichment programs, and accelerated courses of study. The scores themselves can provide valuable information for schools and families attempting to understand and meet the needs of gifted students and plan for their futures.

National Spelling Bee

http://www.spellingbee.com

Sponsored by the Scripps Company and popularized in the documentary *Spellbound* (2002), the National Spelling Bee begins at the individual school level; progresses to city, regional, and state competitions; and concludes with the national finals in Washington, DC. Its purpose is to help students improve spelling, increase vocabularies, and develop correct English usage.

Odyssey of the Mind

http://odysseyofthemind.com

Similar to Destination ImagiNation, this program teaches problem solving and creative thinking and builds self-confidence, interpersonal skills, and creativity. Students work in groups and teams to solve long- and short-term problems. Local teams progress to regional, state, and national competitions.

The Scholastic Art & Writing Awards

http://www.scholastic.com/artandwritingawards

Students in grades 7–12 can submit writing and art to this national competition. They receive evaluations, ratings, and awards.

Science Olympiad

http://www.soinc.org

The Science Olympiad offers two divisions appropriate for middle school students: Division A2 (grades 3–6) and Division B (grades 6–9). Tournaments are designed to demonstrate students' understanding and mastery of concepts in science, mathematics, and technology. Students display knowledge and solve problems both individually and as a team. Competitions are local, regional, statewide, and national.

The WordMasters Challenge

http://www.wordmasterschallenge.com

This unusual national competition for students in grades 3–8 encourages vocabulary development, higher level word comprehension, logical thinking, and verbal reasoning through analogies.

Summer Programs

For many gifted students, even the finest public or private schools cannot provide enough. For them, summer programs, distance learning, and community resources are necessary, as they provide additional interaction with university faculty, professional artists, and other gifted students on a broader scale than their local school can provide. Students make contact with others who provide social support for learning and achievement at challenging levels. Exposure to more demanding content also helps improve study skills and can decrease underachieving behaviors that are the result of too much work that is easy and therefore boring (Rimm, 1991).

Residential summer programs help develop independence and living skills. Students experience a slice of college and university life, which helps raise their educational goals (Davis & Rimm, 2004). These programs are especially beneficial during the critical middle school years when most students are not yet old enough to work, but have outgrown their summer camps.

Community programs such as those offered through local art or natural history museums, zoos, historical societies, cooperative extension, and garden centers can provide additional experiences for gifted students. They also introduce students to local adults who share their interests and who can perhaps become mentors and role models. In the arts, especially, expert mentors are essential for full talent development.

Many colleges and universities offer programming in special interest areas, as well as advanced academics, often for high school credit. The following is a list of some of the better known university programs, although specific information about courses, activities and programming is available on the Web sites and may change annually.

Gifted Education Resource Institute (GERI) Summer Residential Camps at Purdue University (grades 5–12)
http://www.geri.soe.purdue.edu/youth/default.html

The Junior Scholars Academy at the Belin-Blank Center for Gifted and Talented Development, University of Iowa (grades 6–8)
http://www.continuetolearn.uiowa.edu/ccp/summer/gifted_education.htm

The Academic Talent Development Program at the University of California, Berkeley (ages 11–17)
http://atdp.berkeley.edu

The Duke University Talent Identification Program (grades 7–10)
http://www.tip.duke.edu/ss/ss.htm
Duke TIP offers students the opportunity to learn highly challenging material at a rate suited to their advanced abilities. Students enroll in a single Duke TIP-designed course for 3 weeks of in-depth study.

The Center for Talented Youth at Johns Hopkins University
http://www.jhu.edu/gifted/ctysummer
Available on university campuses throughout the country, CTY offers 3-week residential programs during which students have intense immersion in just one course. In addition, there are social, arts, and sports experiences outside the classroom.

Northwestern University's Center for Talent Development Spectrum (grades 7–9) and Apogee (grades 4–6) Programs
http://www.ctd.northwestern.edu/summer/description.html
These residential programs are available in multiple locations across the country. Students take enrichment or acceleration courses taught by master teachers and participate in extracurricular activities.

The Summer Institute for the Gifted (grades K–11)
http://www.giftedstudy.com
This is a 3-week summer experience for gifted students held on various college campuses across the East and Midwest.

The Summer Enrichment Program for the Gifted and Talented at the University of Northern Colorado (grades 5–10)
http://www.unco.edu/sep
> This is a 2-week residential summer program that focuses on enrichment not available in regular classrooms.

Yunasa Summer Institute (ages 10–15)
http://www.educationaladvancement.org/programs/students/yunasa/overview
> The goal of this unique, week-long camp experience is for highly gifted middle school students to have fun while developing the emotional, spiritual, physical, and intellectual components of their lives. Faculty include nationally known experts in gifted education.

Because many gifted students are anxious to learn more about and be involved in science, technology, and computers, there are a variety of specific programs targeted for this interest. Three of note are:

Cybercamps (ages 7–18)
http://www.cybercamps.com
> These single and multiweek computer camps are offered on college campuses in 16 states and Washington, DC.

National Computer Camps (ages 8–18)
http://www.nccamp.com
> This camp offers residential or day programs in Connecticut, Georgia, and Ohio.

Space Camp (ages 9–11 and 12–14)
http://www.spacecamp.com
> Six- and 13-day experiences are available for ages 12–14 in California, Florida, and Alabama. There are also 3- and 6-day programs for ages 9–11. Participants engage in simulations

and experiences that teach them to think and act like astronauts. Simulated missions to a space station and crew rotation highlight the courses. In the advanced academies, there are three tracks: Space, Aviation, and Robotics.

Students with musical, athletic, dramatic, or other artistic talent need the constant challenge and support of expert coaching and teaching in their particular field. Rarely will a school or district have this at a deep enough level. Programs like Interlochen Arts Camp in Michigan (http://www.interlochen.org/camp) or the School of Cinema and Performing Arts (http://www.socapa.org/hs/hs) with campuses in New York City, Hollywood, and the Massachusetts Berkshires can provide opportunities for students to have an intense experience in their talent area.

The Web site of the National Association for Gifted Children (http://www.nagc.org/summer/intro.html) lists summer programs by region of the United States, as well as international offerings. An extensive list of summer programs for gifted students organized by national and international programs, as well as by state, is also available at Hoagie's Gifted Education Page (http://www.hoagiesgifted.org/summer.htm).

Several misconceptions may keep students away from participation in summer programs (Schatz & Schuster, 1996). Students may express concern that they don't want to spend the summer with "a bunch of nerds." However, gentle coaxing and word-of-mouth testimonials from previous participants can help overcome these fears of being labeled "uncool" for a summer spent with academic or artistic activities. Parents are sometimes concerned that these are "genius" camps and that their youngster isn't bright enough. However, careful examination of the requirements for each program, thoughtful teacher recommendations, and evaluations of students' above-grade-level performance in particular areas can match students with appropriate-level experiences. The third misconception involves cost, namely that summer programs are very expensive. This is sometimes true, but many programs have sliding scales and scholarships available, and gifted teachers and coordinators may have information about state and local gifted groups that provide support for summer experiences. Commuter programs cost less than residential ones, but offer less opportunity for social and emotional growth. The investment value of these summer programs is reflected in consistent rave reviews from the majority of student participants and the positive influence of these experiences on their lives.

When students return home after these exceptionally stimulating and rewarding summer experiences, there can be issues of continuity and resistance. Students may abruptly and painfully realize the limitations of their school and even of their peers. Thoughtful counseling and patience may be necessary to help them make a smooth transition when they return in the fall.

Distance Learning

Another option for students, either during the school year or during the summer, is distance learning. One advantage of this approach is that it can be arranged around students' other activities (e.g., music or sports camps, work, family responsibilities). A wide range of opportunities for enrichment and advancement are available through correspondence courses and via the Internet. Extensive lists are available at Hoagies's Gifted Education Page (http://www.hoagiesgifted.org/distance_learning.htm) and at the Institute for Educational Advancement's Gifted Resource Center (http://www.educationaladvancement.org/resources/search/learning.php), which also has listings of contests, awards, and scholarships. AP classes are available online, as well as other junior and senior high school honors classes. The Center for Talented Youth at Johns Hopkins University, the Center for Talent Development at Northwestern University, and Educational Programs for Gifted Youth (EPGY) at Stanford University together sponsor distance learning for gifted K–8 students in math, physics, and writing, with credit offered by Stanford and Johns Hopkins. The Center for Talent Development also offers Learning Links, correspondence courses in a wider range of subject areas. The Institute for Mathematics and Computer Science (IMACS) offers online interactive math and computer science curricula for talented middle and high school students. Many other online courses and programs that may offer high school or college credit are available in individual states. With the growth of home-schooling and improvements in technology, more and more of these options are available every year. It is important for parents and teachers to screen offerings to be sure they are accredited and reputable.

Students who get the most benefit from these experiences are self-motivated and have assistance structuring their time to complete the courses. Sometimes, a mentor or tutor is necessary in case students get "stuck," either with the process or the content. These are usually available through the online instructor, but not always.

The Duke University Talent Identification Program (http://www.tip.duke.edu/IL/Independent-Learning.htm) also offers independent, individual enrichment courses in two formats: CD-ROM enrichment and TIP materials. Students use TIP materials to explore a topic of interest at their own pace with help and guidance from a mentor with expertise in the content area. Courses at two grade levels are available: TIP Learn on Your Own (LOYO) for grades 5–11 and Duke TIP MAPacks for grades 4–6.

Through the Internet, students can expand their knowledge, connect with master teachers and experts, and expand their classmates and friends throughout the nation and world. These benefits, plus those of self-pacing and intellectual challenge, can make distance learning a powerful component of the education of self-motivated gifted students. It is also a particularly useful tool for students in small or rural schools where honors and advanced coursework may not be available.

Community and Social Service

Because of gifted children's heightened moral sensitivity and sense of fairness and justice, social and community service opportunities may add to feelings of self-worth and efficacy—the belief that they can make a difference. These activities allow adolescents to develop problem-solving strategies, explore social issues and new ideas, gain exposure to role models and possible mentors, and help shape their identities (Jackson & Davis, 2000). Service learning is often a part of middle school advisory programs and curricula, and its prevalence in middle schools is increasing (Jackson & Davis). Such involvement is also encouraged by gifted experts, who emphasize the responsibilities to society that gifted individuals share:

> More and more it becomes clear that human welfare on the whole is much more a matter of the activities of *deviates* than it is a matter of what the middle mass of persons does. (Hollingworth cited in Ward, 1980, p. 42)

> The best function of exceptionally high abilities is to perform valuable services which no lesser ability can perform at all. . . . From the moment that a man or a woman has demonstrated his possession of such ability, society should, in its own interests, arrange that he does for it what only he and his kind can do. (Thorndike cited in Ward, 1980, p. 43)

> The gifted must be deliberately educated for participation in, and the advancement of, world culture. (Ward, 1980, p. 67)

Students find community service activities most valuable to them when they are provided with structured opportunities to reflect on and evaluate their experiences. Both the service and reflection can be built into gifted and middle school programs with the support and guidance of teachers, counselors, parents, and community members. Social and community service activities can also be part of leadership development in middle school advisory or gifted programs. A variety of curricular materials and training programs are available that help students identify personal traits of leaders and themselves, study leaders of the past and present, establish goals, and implement plans for local problem-solving projects.

Next Steps . . . Taking Action

1. Determine what academic competitions and clubs already exist at your school. Explore those that would add new directions. Consider sources for funding and coaching (e.g., faculty, parents, community members).

2. Be sure academic competitions and clubs are available to all students in the school with the interest and ability to participate regardless of formal gifted identification.

3. Help guidance counselors be aware of summer opportunities, online courses, distance learning, and acceleration possibilities so that these can be included in scheduling conferences and counseling meetings for gifted students.

4. Communicate regularly with parents and students about opportunities, especially those outside of the school or community. Panels of students who have participated can help break down negative stereotypes and allay fears.

5. Work with individual students to match interests and needs with opportunities.

6. Work with district-level personnel, parents, and community resources to develop needed accelerated and enriched summer and weekend opportunities within your own school and district.

References

Brody, L. E., & Stanley, J. C. (1991). Young college students: Assessing factors that contribute to success. In W. T. Southern & E. D. Jones (Eds.), *The academic acceleration of gifted children* (pp. 102–132). New York: Teachers College Press.

Davis, G. A., & Rimm, S. B. (2004). *Education of the gifted and talented* (5th ed.). Boston: Allyn and Bacon.

Feldhusen, J. (1991). Saturday and summer programs. In N. Colangelo & G. A. Davis (Eds.), *Handbook of gifted education* (pp. 197–208). Boston: Allyn and Bacon.

Jackson, A. W., & Davis, G. A. (2000). *Turning points 2000: Educating adolescents in the 21st century.* New York: Teachers College Press.

Karnes, F. A., & Riley, T. L. (2005). *Competitions for talented kids.* Waco, TX: Prufrock Press.

Piskurich, P. (2003). The role of summer programs. In J. F. Smutny (Ed.), *Designing and developing programs for gifted students* (pp. 129–137). Thousand Oaks, CA: Corwin Press.

Rimm, S. (1991). Underachievement and superachievement: Flip sides of the same psychological coin. In N. Colangelo & G. A. Davis (Eds.), *Handbook of gifted education* (2nd ed., pp. 416–434). Boston: Allyn and Bacon.

Schatz, E., & Schuster, N. (1996). *Teens with talent: Developing the potential of the bright, brighter, and brightest.* Boulder, CO: Open Space Communications.

Ward, V. S. (1980). *Differential education for the gifted.* Los Angeles: National/ State Leadership Training Institute on the Gifted and the Talented.

Additional Resources

DeLong, M. R., & Howel, W. C. (Eds.). (1995). *Full potential: A guide for parents of bright teens.* Durham, NC: Duke University Talent Identification Program.

Olszewski-Kubilius, P. (1997). Special summer and Saturday programs for gifted students. In N. Colangelo & G. A. Davis (Eds.), *Handbook of gifted education* (2nd ed., pp. 180–188). Boston: Allyn and Bacon.

Afterword

I t's hard to close this book. I've spent more than 20 years working with gifted middle school students, their parents, and teachers, as well as other professionals in the field across the nation. The more I read while I was writing, the more I learned and the more respect I developed for people accepting the challenging mission faced by both fields—that is, to change the nature of schools to make them better places for middle school students and for gifted students. Advocates in both fields feel intensely driven by high ideals and values and the potential cost to society of their failure. What if middle schools don't succeed in creating environments that turn kids on to personally relevant, challenging intellectual pursuits? What if the many sensitivities, talents, and abilities of gifted students aren't nurtured and developed? What will the future be like for all of them . . . and all of us?

I hope that this book has helped establish common ground for continuing conversation and action in middle schools. I find this quote from R. H. Blyth encouraging and reassuring: "Perfect does not mean perfect actions in a perfect world, but appropriate actions in an imperfect one." We just need to keep going!

I keep wondering, "What else can I share with readers that might help them? Reassure them? Encourage them? Inform their actions? Change the way middle schools 'do business'?" What else do you need or want to know? Please e-mail me with questions, suggestions, comments, personal experiences, and the like. Maybe there'll be a revision or a second volume that answers your questions and concerns or presentations at NAGC or NMSA. I look forward to hearing from you.

—Susan
susanrakow@earthlink.net

NMSA/NAGC Joint Position Statement

**Meeting the Needs of High Ability and High Potential
Learners in the Middle Grades:
A Joint Position Statement of the National Middle School
Association and the National Association for Gifted Children**

The National Association for Gifted Children and the National Middle School Association share a commitment to developing schools and classrooms in which both equity and excellence are persistent goals for each learner. Equity refers to the opportunity of every learner to have supported access to the highest possible quality education. Excellence refers to the need of every learner for opportunities and adult support necessary to maximize his or her learning potential.

Early adolescence is generally described as the time between ages 10 and 15. During this developmental span, young adolescents experience a wide range of growth rates in cognitive, physical, social, emotional, and moral dimensions. Change in young adolescents can be rapid and uneven. In addition to the diversity of development implicit in early adolescence, middle schools also reflect diversity in student gender, culture, experience, economic status, interests, and learning preferences. Every middle school classroom also represents a wide array of talents.

In light of the inevitable variance in middle school populations, it is critical that middle school educators develop increasing awareness of and skill necessary to address the full range of learner needs—including needs of those who already demonstrate advanced academic abilities and those who have the potential to work at advanced levels.

High-ability adolescents may differ from fellow classmates in cognitive skills, interests, modes of learning, and motivation. As a result, their educational needs may also differ in some important ways from those of other young adolescents. Attending to those needs requires informed attention to both equity and excellence in all facets of schooling.

Identification

All middle school learners need educators who consistently use both formal and informal means of recognizing their particular strengths and needs. In regard to advanced learners, identification requires specific plans to seek out students with advanced abilities or advanced potential in order to provide appropriate educational experiences during the transition into adolescence. Both the National Middle School Association and the National Association for Gifted Children share a strong commitment to appropriate use of multiple approaches to identify high potential in students from minority and low-economic groups. Identification of high performance and potential are precursors to helping young adolescents maximize their potential during these critical years. Identification of student performance and potential should be followed by educational planning to maximize the potential.

Assessment

Ongoing assessment is critical to informing classroom practice. Preassessment, in-process assessments, and post assessments should give learners consistent opportunity to demonstrate their knowledge, understanding, and skill related to topics of study.

Assessments related to student readiness, interests, perspectives, and learning preferences provide educators with a consistently emerging understanding of each learner's needs in the classroom. Middle level educators should use data from such assessments to modify teaching and learning plans to ensure that each student— including those who already perform well beyond expectations— have consistent opportunities to extend their abilities.

Curriculum and Instruction

Equity in the middle grades requires that all learners have an opportunity to participate in curriculum that is rich in meaning and focused on thought and application. Excellence requires support necessary to show continual growth in knowledge, understanding, and skill. Advanced middle grade learners thus require consistent opportunities to work at degrees of challenge somewhat beyond their particular readiness levels, with support necessary to achieve at the new levels of proficiency. In addition, educators should address student interests and preferred modes of learning in planning curriculum and instruction that is appropriately challenging for individual learners. Educational resources should be of a sufficient range of complexity to ensure challenge for advanced learners. Flexible pacing and flexible grouping arrangements are important instructional adjustments for many highly able middle level learners. Because of the inevitable variance among high-ability learners, advanced learners, like other middle school students, need curriculum and instruction proactively designed to accommodate their particular needs.

Affective Development

Critical to healthy development in the middle grade years is development of positive student affect. Students benefit greatly from learning environments that reinforce their worth as individuals and simultaneously support them in becoming more powerful and productive. For advanced learners, this may require helping students affirm both their abilities and their need to belong to a peer group. Middle level educators need to understand and address the unique dynamics that high-ability and high-potential young adolescents may experience as they seek to define themselves and their roles among peers.

Effective Partnerships

Building a middle school culture that supports equity and excellence for each learner requires sustained attention to partnerships among all adults key to the student's development. This includes partnerships between home and school, specialists and generalists, and teachers and administrators. Middle level schools should assist parents in recognizing, understanding, and nurturing advanced abilities and potential in young adolescents. Partnerships among team members and between classroom teachers and gifted education specialists should ensure appropriate challenge for advanced learners and appropriate attention to the particular talents of advanced learners. Administrator/teacher partnerships should define what it means to accommodate the individual needs of learners and develop conditions that lead to such accommodations for all middle level learners—including those who demonstrate advanced performance or potential.

Pre-Service and In-Service Staff Development

To ensure equity and excellence in the middle grades, teachers must be adequately prepared to provide academically rich instruction for all students and to teach in ways that enable all students to work at appropriate and escalating levels of challenge. Teachers with training in gifted education are more likely to foster high-level thinking, allow for greater student expression, consider individual variance in their teaching, and understand how to provide high-end challenge. Appropriate staff development for middle level teachers will continually focus on high-quality curriculum, understanding and teaching in response to individual as well as group needs, and developing a repertoire of instructional strategies that support and manage flexible classrooms. Central to the success of these endeavors is shared responsibility for meeting the needs of each learner, evidenced in systematic and consistent planning, carrying out of plans, and evaluation of effectiveness of plans in terms of individual learners and small groups of learners as well as the class as a whole.

With these shared beliefs, the National Association for Gifted Children and the National Middle School Association call on middle level educators to adopt and support processes and actions that ensure developmentally appropriate practices for the full range of students they serve.

A Call to Action

The National Association for Gifted Children and the National Middle School Association urge administrators, teachers, gifted education specialists, school support personnel, parents, and students to collaborate for the purpose of ensuring equity and excellence for all learners, including those with advanced performance or potential.

District and School Leaders Should:
1. Provide leadership in creating a school climate that vigorously supports both equity and excellence.
2. Ensure that teachers have meaningful knowledge and understanding about the needs of gifted adolescents, including training in differentiated instruction so that the needs of all students—including those with advanced performance or potential—are appropriately addressed.
3. Develop and implement an appropriate and flexible system for identifying high-ability learners from diverse populations.
4. Use organizational structures such as teaming and advisory programs to ensure that needs of young adolescents, including high-ability young adolescents, are central in instructional planning.

5. Encourage consistent collaboration among all teachers and support personnel in the school to ensure appropriate services for high-ability learners.
6. Ensure a continuum of services including options such as differentiation, advanced classes, acceleration, short-term seminars, independent studies, mentorships and other learning opportunities matched to the varied needs of high-potential and high-ability learners.
7. Provide counseling-related services for students with advanced academic performance or potential.
8. Develop and maintain a written plan to guide educational planning for advanced learners and to inform the community of those plans.
9. Regularly evaluate the effectiveness of curriculum, instruction, resources, and other services in supporting the development of high-ability learners.

Teachers, Gifted Education Specialists, and Support Personnel Should:
1. Be knowledgeable about students with advanced academic abilities and those who have the potential to work at advanced levels.
2. Meet regularly to discuss the needs of all students, including those with high ability.
3. Provide curriculum, instruction, and other opportunities to meet the needs of students with high ability.
4. Use a variety of developmentally appropriate instructional practices to enable each student to experience a high degree of personal excellence.
5. Collaborate with colleagues at elementary and high school levels to ensure a smooth transition as students progress throughout the grades.
6. Keep parents informed about their children's growth and invite parent participation in educational planning for their children.

Parents Should:
1. Strengthen family connections with young adolescents.
2. Be knowledgeable about the needs and concerns of young, gifted adolescents.
3. Understand and contribute to the district's plan for identifying and serving high-ability learners.
4. Help their children take appropriate responsibility for their own learning and develop related skills and attitudes of responsible independence.
5. Collaborate with the school to ensure that their children's needs are being met.
6. Be their children's best advocates.

The Salem Witch Trials Unit

by Katie Anderson
Wiley Middle School, University Heights, OH

Topic:
   The Salem Witch Trials, Eighth-Grade Social Studies

Time Frame:
   1 week

Goals:
   My goals are to encourage students to view the witch trials from multiple perspectives and to recognize the role that the early American government played in this atrocity. I would also like students to recognize how the trials aided in the evolution of the American ideal of freedom of religion.

Specific Objectives/Standards:
   • *People in Societies 1:* Analyze how the concept of religious freedom has evolved in the U.S.
   • *People in Societies 2*: Describe and explain the social, economic, and political effects of institutionalized racism and discrimination.
   • *Government 6:* Explain how specific provisions of the U.S. Constitution, including the Bill of Rights, limit the powers of government in order to protect the rights of individuals with emphasis on freedom of religion. (This will

be a point that leads us into the Bill of Rights Unit later in the semester.)

- *Social Studies Skills and Methods 4*: Organize and lead a discussion.

Lesson Procedures and Activities:

Two weeks prior to beginning of lesson, preassess students' knowledge with a quiz, including: What were the Salem Witch Trials? Whose fault was it that people were killed? Can you think of any other time in American history where innocent people were killed by the government?

Monday: (Background Information) Introduction of the Salem Witch Trials. Teacher will lecture and write notes on overhead about basic background information. Students will add to discussion based on their own background knowledge and will write appropriate notes. Teacher will show scenes from the film version of *The Crucible* with particular emphasis on the courthouse scenes to engage students' interest.

Tuesday: (Jigsaw) Students will be assigned an article to read in class. After reading their article, students will be placed into groups with others who have read their article. Students will summarize the article together and discuss important points. Students will jot down their own notes for later use in Jigsaw.

Primary Resources will be given out as follows:
- Students who answered zero or one out of the three questions correctly on the pretest will read *A Minister's View* and *Sarah Good's Trial* along with guided reading questions (http://www.digitalhistory. uh.edu/historyonline/us5.cfm)
- Students who answered two of the questions correctly will read *Rebecca Nurse's Pre-Trial Examination* (http:// www.iath.virginia.edu/salem/people/nursecourt.html)